Ornette C

JAZZ MASTERS SERIES

Ornette Coleman

BARRY McRAE

Selected Discography by
Tony Middleton

For Stuart Behn

First published in Great Britain in 1988 by
APOLLO PRESS LIMITED
11 Baptist Gardens, London NW5 4ET

© Barry McRae 1988

British Library Cataloguing in Publication Data
McRae, Barry
   Ornette Coleman.—(Jazz masters series; v.14).
   1. Coleman, Ornette   2. Jazz musicians—
   United States—Biography
   I. Title   II. Middleton, Tony   III. Series
   785.42′092′4   ML419.C63

ISBN 0-948820-08-X

Series editor: David Burnett James

Printed and Bound in Great Britain by
Anchor Brendon Limited, Tiptree, Essex

Contents

Illustrations

Introduction

In a chequered history of well under one hundred years, jazz has taken three major changes of direction. The first turned the collective music of New Orleans into a solo art form. The second ushered jazz beyond the concept of melodic improvisation, while the third eschewed formal structure as a basis for the music. None of these changes came about because of a single musician, yet each had a central figure, one who brought his talents to bear on the problems involved in a very special way. Trumpeter Louis Armstrong, perhaps the most important of the three, gave jazz a solo language and, as early as 1924, was producing solos of a grandeur previously unknown. Alto saxophonist Charlie Parker became the lodestone of the bebop movement in the middle forties. He was the leader of those who provided a blueprint for the building of new tunes on old and established chord sequences. The third, also an altoist, was Ornette Coleman and he became the driving force within a coterie of musicians who avoided all use of pre-determined structure.

Coleman was far from being the first man to essay this difficult task. Pianist Lennie Tristano had already demonstrated what could be done in this direction. Coleman, however, was the first to give the new style a valid grammar of its own. For once the jingoists were right and the term 'free form' was an acceptable description of how the Coleman group of musicians actually played.

It was a style that was pure melody. Excellent themes were produced and these were then used as launching pads for free blowing. The harmonies of the theme did not direct the solos and only oblique reference was made to them. It was a style that was to attract a whole new generation of jazzmen and was to introduce new tonalities into the fabric of jazz.

Coleman's rewards were meagre but he remained a steadfast experimentalist. He returned from a two year sabbatical in the sixties having added the playing of violin and trumpet to his instrumental skills. He also showed his ability as a classical composer, producing several chamber works as well as writing for a full orchestra.

He continued to tour world-wide with an excellent jazz group and it was not until the middle seventies that he took another decisive step. Finding himself in a rock orientated world, he brought his own special skills to the task of finding an acceptable niche for himself. The outcome was 'harmolodic' jazz, a method in which the return to rhythmic and harmonic orthodoxy was tempered by the need to stay 'free'. Pulse and metre were stabilized but the top strata retained the licence of earlier styles. It was a change of direction that was to take us through to the Ornette Coleman of today (1988).

When will the Blues leave?

Ornette Coleman was born in Fort Worth on March 9th, 1930. Cowtown, as befits the town that was once the home of the largest stockyards in the U.S., was situated in an area of farmland close to the rich Texas oil and gas fields. It had a thriving clothing industry, a tradition for making military uniforms and, by the forties, a population that had reached several hundred thousands.

It was something of an open town and the presence of local people employed in the textile industry, the regular influx of manual oil workers and the flamboyant Texan spirit made it a colourful place to live. Like many provincial towns of its kind, it had its poor and the Coleman family were among them. To make matters worse, Coleman Senior had died in 1937, leaving his son to be brought up by his widow and her sister.

Despite this, life was not all bad and music was a considerable consolation to a socially deprived youngster. He told A.B. Spellman[4] that 'I used to go around in the neighbourhood and hear guys playing kazoos and various kinds of odd instruments, making up all kinds of music, but I didn't really get into any kind of music myself until my first year at High School'.

Coleman certainly did not involve himself with these amateur 'spasm bands' and his contact with real instruments came about through his cousin James Jordan, who played reed instruments and taught music in Austin, a Texan town some miles to the south. While staying at the Coleman houshold he would leave his instrument around and the temptation to dabble was too great for the young teenager.

By playing along with records, Ornette began to fathom the rudiments of the horn and when, at fourteen, his mother was finally able to afford an alto, he knew at least a little of its mechanics. Nevertheless, the youngster was not prepared to muddle along and he admired Jordan's own attention to detail. As his interest in music increased, he set out to match the tonal accuracy and clean articulation displayed by his relative.

In view of later events, this was not without its ironical aspect but the young Coleman had begun to study elementary harmony and to read as many musical theory books as he could find. He had also moved over to the tenor saxophone and taken a place in the school band. Also in the line-up was Curtis Ousley, who later gained fame as King Curtis and divided his activities between jazz and being a highly successful r and b figure. At the time, Coleman saw little reason to distinguish between the two styles but it was because of playing in a jazz-based manner that he was invited by his music teacher to leave the band.

It was of little consequence to him at the time because he was playing in the black r and b clubs and he was just pleased to be involved in his town's very active blues scene. Disc-jockeys like Doctor Jazzbo were pumping out blues on Station KFJZ day and night and there were clubs to satisfy most blues tastes. The impressionable Coleman was still at school and was performing, in the main, without parental acquiescence, although keeping his nocturnal activities secret was not easy. Fortunately, the money he earned helped to support the family budget and gradually his mother began to turn a blind eye.

This made his progress easier and he happily embraced the blues club jive. His playing was built around heavy blues riffs and his idols were Louis Jordan and Arnett Cobb. He had his hair 'conked', got himself a Zoot suit, *the* outfit of the time (and place), and he showed himself willing to adopt the gymnastic contortions required in blues club 'crowd baiting'. Inevitably, Coleman's r and b activities of the period deflected him from his interest in jazz in its more pure form although, on one occasion, he actually sat in with the Stan Kenton Orchestra. It was his meeting with Red Connors, however, that redressed the balance. The man was something of a local hero and had actually played with Charlie Parker, although claims that he was a saxophonist to compare with Sonny Rollins and John Coltrane have little, save hearsay, to support them.

Coleman certainly thought that there was more than a grain of truth in them and it was, in fact, Connors who convinced the youngster to take bebop seriously. They actually played on jobs together when possible and, although Coleman broadened his bop repertoire, he stayed loyal to the tenor on the money-earning blues gigs.

His career for a period began to move along two distinctly parallel tracks, one driven by the empirical bebop thinker and the other by the reasonably successful, young r and b player. It was not a situation that really suited him but it was expedient. He enjoyed playing alto with Red Connors in white jazz clubs but also played tenor with Connors' bands at local dances, where the demand was unequivocally for the blues. He also assembled his own small bands when the occasion demanded and got a considerable lift from backing the likes of Big Joe Turner in blues joints.

He was, however, already getting some resistance because of the unconventional way in which he played and because of his increasingly non-conformist appearance. Inevitably, it was his music that caused most concern. He felt that he played on the natural pitch of the instrument and told Valerie Wilmer[8] that 'he believed that every human being had a "non tempered" psyche.'

Certainly, such ideas would have seemed like gibberish to a simple, practising blues musician. Conviction can easily sound like an excuse in such circumstances and Coleman began to experience increasing antipathy towards his highly personal sense of pitch. For his part, he was somewhat resentful at such blinkered attitudes but his more serious gripe was with Fort Worth and its claustrophobic, racial and social mores. It was a time to leave, and the nineteen year old Coleman joined a touring carnival with Silas Green from New Orleans. At least it settled one aspect of his musical quandary. The Green entourage played tent shows and small Negro theatres and made a virtue out of playing 'nothin' but the blues'. In reality, even this was not true and the Green 'book' included about every trite tune known to man.

It is possible that Coleman made his first recording on this tour, although some confusion has arisen about the details. He told

Spellman[4] that in 1949 he had recorded while on tour with Green. *A Discography Of Free Jazz** by Erik Raben (Karl Emil Knudsen) agreed that it was 1949 but averred that it had been with the Clarence Samuels' r and b band. In fact, both nearly had it right. The session had taken place in Natchez during the Green tour but he told this writer that it had been with Clarence Samuels' rhythm section *only*. In view of the quality of the music involved, it hardly seems to matter but what is certain is that it was in Natchez that Green fired Coleman for introducing his 'jazz ways' into the band.

Worse was to follow, and after a run-in with the local constabulary, the young saxophonist was advised that Natchez had all the musicians it could handle and that he had best leave town. In fairness, it must be said that he would have cut a strange figure with his slight frame and extremely heavy beard and that strangers would have had some justification for eyeing him with suspicion.

It is perhaps fortunate that he was something of a loner because it allowed him to travel light and it was not long before he landed a job with the better known Clarence Samuels (hence the recording dilemma). He worked with the band for several months but life continued to be precarious. He told Spellman (sleeve note: *Ornette On Tenor*) 'I was in this place in Baton Rouge, playing with this blues singer and this guy came up and told me there were people outside that wanted to meet me. I went out there and these cats were big. They said "goddamit, we don't like musicians" and started beating my ass. But I tried to protect my horn by holding it in both arms and I tried to protect my face with the case, and they prised my arms apart and one of them took my horn and threw it off the hill just like you throw a bottle on some rocks. It didn't have anything to do with me or my music'.

Despite that closing statement, the incident did have quite an effect on him and, when Samuels reached New Orleans, the 'saxophonist without a saxophone' left the band. In fact, he remained in the city for more than six months and, in particular, befriended clarinettist Alvin Batiste and drummer Ed Blackwell. Unfortunately, he could not get regular, musical work and he spent most of that time in manual employment, taking any odd playing engagement that might offer itself and then, with the aid of a borrowed horn. This way of life was no physical hardship because he was young and fit, but it did temporarily blight his ambition.

This disillusionment was made even greater when he faced rejection from local jazz musicians. Criticism from the artisans of the r and b world was acceptable but, from his peers, it was a different matter. Could it be that his strangely idiosyncratic style was without merit? Did he change the rules too drastically? These were questions he had to answer himself. Certainly he found it very hard to accept the fact that established, modern players were prepared to pack up and leave, rather than jam with him.

Nevertheless, his most immediate problem was to get out of New Orleans and, on discovering that Pee Wee Crayton was passing through on route to record in Los Angeles, joined him for the trip. He had worked with Crayton in Fort Worth and had, at the time, performed to the leader's satisfaction. In theory, it should have worked again, the tour was brief and Coleman had always seemed able to compromise.

It did not work out like that, however. The germ of the new Coleman style had really begun to mature, as had his conviction that he should be his own man. He had outgrown bebop in its purest form or perhaps, in truth, had never really come to terms with it. Set against this, he could not totally ignore the emotional charge that he got from the blues bands. He was at the stage when his style was something of a hybrid and he was looking for ways in which he could introduce his theories into the musical environment in which he found himself.

Connie Curtis Crayton, for his part, was an old time blues entertainer but he was no bigot. In the late forties he had recorded with Harry 'Sweets' Edison's Orchestra. In the early fifties he had worked with the Red Callender Sextet, with Bumps Myers on tenor, and his own 1956/7 unit had included a saxophone team of Red Holloway and McKinley Easton. This hardly made him an experimentalist, however, and he had little sympathy for Coleman's enquiring stance.

Audience reaction was the most vital element for him and it did not take long for him to realise that this new saxophonist was making few friends on the blues circuit. Coleman later told Nat Hentoff (sleeve note: *Something Else!*) 'He didn't understand what I was trying to do and it got so that he was paying me not to play.'

The truth was that more likely he did know, at least to some extent, but did not want the radical young man's music in *his* band.

Unfortunately, it was a story that was later latched upon by Coleman's opponents to prove his 'incompetence'. It was, of course, just the opposite but it rapidly led to the altoist again being away from home and without a job.

Tomorrow is the Question

The only difference was that he was now in Los Angeles and he moved into the Morris Hotel, an ageing hotel frequented by musicians and artists. At first, he was able to survive on gigs in and around the city but the chromatic licence that he had begun to take did not endear him to the 'technique conscious' Californians. The New Orleans' situation repeated itself and he became unwelcome, even at 'after hours' sessions.

Coleman became increasingly unhappy, there were one or two unpleasant incidents at the Morris, the bosom of his home town beckoned and, toward the end of 1952, he returned to Fort Worth. There was the added incentive that his good friend, drummer Charles Moffett was due to get married and, after making known his intentions to return, Coleman was invited to be best man.

It was a happy occasion and it represented something of a reunion with many old friends. Much of the talk was about music and almost inevitably a jam session developed after the ceremony. In the course of it, Coleman locked horns with fellow saxophonist Leo Wright and trumpeter Bobby Bradford who was present (Richard Williams' interview in the *Melody Maker*, 17 July 1971) described it as a rare, musical experience. 'It was really great, like the old gunfights, but nothing malicious. We were trying to find out which of them was the baddest alto player and, at the end of it all, the concensus was that it was Ornette all the way'.

Bradford went on to say 'Ornette was already getting that sound of his own – like Bird (Charlie Parker) and Sonny (Rollins) would use the device of playing half a step above the key for one phrase, just to add piquancy, but Ornette would go out and stay there – he wouldn't come back after one phrase, and this would test the listener's capacity for accepting dissonance. '

Regrettably, such impromptu sessions still represented Coleman's best opportunity to play jazz but, although he was restless, it was an endurable existence. Perhaps the biggest drawback was that many of his former, musical associates had left town, themselves alienated by the lack of real work opportunities. The altoist again found himself alone in a 'Coleman versus the World' situation but decided that, at least, he should select the site for the battle. He returned to California but not to the Morris. He moved in with a friend in Watts, a ghetto area of downtown Los Angeles.

Things had not improved, musically, on the West Coast, however, and Coleman became more introspective about his own situation. He grew more and more facial hair and continued to dress in eccentric clothes. He seemed determined to be accepted on only his own terms and even his friends dubbed him a black Jesus figure. He represented the complete antithesis of the clean cut, Hollywood High School undershirt and tidy crew cut image of the cool jazz musician.

This was not a policy designed to get him much work nor to make him new friends. Yet, that is exactly what did happen. He met Jayne, an attractive jazz fan, who had heard him play and liked both what she had seen and heard. She was a Jehovah's Witness and herself something of an outlandish dresser and there was an immediate affinity. Within months they were married and, through his new wife, he was introduced to a new circle of musician friends.

He was still regarded as a rather odd figure and approached with trepidation by the establishment players. Even some who had given encouragement during his previous stay had lost patience with his seemingly provocative attitudes and he again found musical employment difficult. In fact, for a period of more than two years he worked as an elevator attendant in a large departmental store. Ironically, this step was to help his musical career, because he took to going to the top floor, switching off the lift and reading an endless stream of musical books. He attests to improving his knowledge of harmony in this way but, after a reasonable period of 'unofficially paid' study, the store decided that their patrons would be happier with a fully automatic elevator.

A chance meeting in a streetcar re-united Coleman with Bradford who had also left Texas. Coleman had begun to compose more seriously and together they practised his tunes. They had also begun to get the odd engagement together and they took the opportunity to slip the occasional original into each set. To Bradford it represented an exercise in re-learning (*Melody Maker*, 17 July 1971) because, he pointed out, 'Ornette doesn't read or write music conventionally – he has his own system of notation, which he teaches to his musicians – and I remember that one time I wrote down that piece, *Chippie*, off his first album on a scrap of paper for him. Several years later, when I saw him in New York, he produced that tiny, scruffy bit of paper again – he'd kept it all that time'.

Regrettably, Coleman's musical studies had not increased his popularity with the majority of local players. To make matters worse, for someone without a regular job, he had become a father, and his regular trumpet partner had just left to join the Air Force. It certainly marked the nadir in his fortunes but it was about this time that he met Don Cherry and from then on the tide turned for him.

Cherry was born in Oklahoma City, where his parents ran the Cherry Blossom Night Club. He had been in Los Angeles since he was four and his mother had bought him his first trumpet when he was twelve. His progress had been good and, once he had fallen in love with the music of Fats Navarro, his devotion to jazz was assured.

His first meeting with Coleman occurred in Watts and it was somewhat strange. He told Nat Hentoff (sleeve note: *Tomorrow Is The Question*) 'he was trying out a 4½ reed. He had long hair and a beard; it was about 90 degrees and he had on an overcoat. I was scared of him.'

Despite this initial apprehension, they became friendly and this meant that Coleman had again found a kindred spirit. Here was another man who quickly grasped the implications of his style and began to work along the same lines. They rehearsed together, began to achieve an encouraging rapport and, perhaps as a defence mechanism, to present consciously an esoteric face. It was as if they were preparing themselves for the day when they could frighten off the fakers in the same way as had the bebop pioneers.

Such days must have seemed a long way off, however, and both men began to wonder if they would ever come. Fortunately, they were not alone and men like saxophonist James Clay, bassist Don

Payne, pianist Paul Bley and drummer Billy Higgins were becoming involved. Bley had been working with the Chet Baker Quartet during 1955 but he had left and settled on the West Coast. There he formed a group that included Billy Higgins and bassist Charlie Haden, two men later to be central figures in the Coleman story.

During 1957, Cherry and Clay co-led a group called the Jazz Messiahs and the trumpeter has acknowledged the extent of Clay's influence and the way in which he played what he heard and felt. Later that year Coleman had taken over from Clay and from that point on he remained the dominating personality in the group.

Vibraphonist Dave Pike had joined Bley in 1956 but, in the early part of 1958, he had been replaced by Coleman and Cherry and the 'prototype' quintet was complete. Coleman made available his 'book', although he was quick to point out that many of the compositions went back more than six years.

In many ways, they had the same edgy neurosis as had the bebop tunes, but they also had about them an impish, almost mocking quality. It was a feeling that they were defying the listener to follow them, while inviting the musicians in the band so to do.

The titles he chose were also of some significance. He did not just write pieces of music; what he wrote had descriptive qualities and portraits, such as *Jayne* for his wife and *Chippie* for Ed Blackwell's son, gave miniature insights into the characters of the dedicatees. He actually said that 'Tunes come very easy to me when I can see a meaning for the tune' (sleeve note by Nat Hentoff: *Something Else!*).

Invisible was so called because of its well hidden tonal centre. *Tears Inside* told of the inner agony of the blues, while *Turnaround* was a twelve bar blues with a minor triad as a turnback. *Lonely Woman* went perhaps a stage further as the listener almost felt the individual woman's estrangement from the world. *The Fifth Of Beethoven* used the opening notes of Ludwig van's Fifth Symphony while the lightly fragmented *Humpty Dumpty* required no king's men to return it to its whole state after the brilliantly broken solo lines by Cherry and the leader.

The Bley Quintet was recorded on one occasion only, and this when they were captured live at the Hillcrest Club in Los Angeles. Ironically, only two Coleman themes were recorded but it is perhaps *Klactoveesedstene* that should attract our attention. For his two first studio dates, Coleman used only his own material but this session gives an opportunity to hear Charlie Parker's famous blues in the hands of a respectful iconoclast.

In fairness to opponents of Coleman at the time, it must be said that the theme statement is despatched in a rather perfunctory manner. The timing is stiff when compared with the lonely, floating air achieved by Miles Davis and Parker on the 1947 Dial. Cherry sounds tense and it is not until Coleman moves into his solo that the rhythm section loosens up. The alto solo itself is outstanding, not by way of being note perfect, but as an affirmation of Coleman's new ideal. Marion Brown said[1] 'When I heard Ornette Coleman, I heard as much bebop and Charlie Parker in him as I know. I said, "Wow! It's another way of doing the same thing."' This it certainly was.

Coleman, however, still had a long way to go. He had plenty of material to play but nowhere publicly to play it. Sessions continued at home and in the houses of his friends until, at one such session, there was a change in their collective fortunes. While playing at Payne's house, they were heard by big band pianist and bassist, Red Mitchell.

Keith Moore Mitchell was a highly respected member of the West Coast musical community. He had played with Woody Herman, Red Norvo and Gerry Mulligan and his musical opinions were well respected. In the event, he only went half way. He was taken by Coleman's compositions but, like so many before him, failed to see the significance of his free approach to soloing. In so doing, he handed the reactionary critics ammunition that they were still firing twenty years later.

Fortunately, he was not entirely honest in his response and, on the strength of the writing, he did encourage Coleman to take some of his pieces to Contemporary label producer Lester Koenig. The recordman's reaction was similar to that of Mitchell, he liked the tunes but was slightly suspicious of the way in which Coleman and Cherry played them. It was perhaps curiosity rather than Koenig's empirical spirit that won the day but, for whatever reason, Coleman was offered a recording opportunity.

The first session was set up and, in three sessions in February and March 1958, Coleman recorded his own compositions with musicians of his own choice. In one sense, it was an Ornette Coleman retrospective, because all of the tunes used had been written in the troubled early fifties. No doubt they had matured, as modification and later additions had been taken on, but they were a revelation.

They showed that the Coleman style had been born far earlier than observers had imagined and the chromatic licence that they exhibited made it very clear why he had been rejected and often humiliated by the establishment West Coast men. The well schooled 'cool jazz' exponents, with their 'at sight' reading skills and well sculptured solo lines would have found Coleman far too primitive although, in fairness, Coleman was not playing as well as was later the case. A lack of working opportunities had inevitably dulled his playing edge but it was his style, per se, that would have offended them.

In the event, the musical outcome of the 1958 sessions was less than ideal. The use of a quintet including a pianist was far from being the perfect set-up. Walter Norris had been one of Coleman's experimental group of players but, when it came to the session, he was not able to integrate the piano with its 'fixed', tonal values, into the chromatic atmosphere of the music.

Bassist Don Payne was similarly uncomfortable. His background, with the big bands of Tommy Alexander and Maynard Ferguson, had not equipped him for the type of rhythmic and harmonic freedom required. The result, despite drummer Billy Higgins' flexible attitudes, was a rather stereotyped pulse. It was one that Coleman and Cherry largely ignored and, although this was a wise course of action, it did leave the feeling that five musicians were pulling in different directions.

This was not, of course, the case and, when the three sessions that made up the group's second album took place, improvements had been made. The piano had been dropped and on the January and February 1959 dates Coleman used Red Mitchell as his bassist and Shelly Manne as his drummer. It would not be true to say that Mitchell abandoned the traditional, harmonic patterns or that Manne was the equal of Higgins. They were, however, an improved and, most certainly, a lighter rhythm team that their three-man predecessor. Manne, one of jazz's most intuitive players, seemed to learn as he went along and, with Mitchell avoiding being dictatorial, they were a more suitable partnership.

Even better was to come. Before the second record's final date, Coleman and Cherry met and played with the Modern Jazz Quartet. They had gone to San Francisco for the express purpose of recruiting MJQ bassist Percy Heath for the March session but had ended up sitting in with the group. Lewis had been immensely impressed with their input into his own group's music and had thrown his weight behind the idea of using Heath for the contemporary date.

In view of the MJQ's own style with its rigid performance guide lines, Heath was, perhaps, an unlikely choice but, in the event, it proved to be a better idea than that of using Mitchell. His effortless duo conversation with Cherry's trumpet on *Tears Inside* was perhaps the one moment when he seemed to fully grasp the implications of the style but, throughout the date, there were examples of his showing a willingness to stand outside the beat and to replace straight theme statement with cunning innuendo.

Reaction to their first record had been mixed, but at least Coleman had made some allies amongst the critical fraternity. In the main, support came from expected quarters with Nat Hentoff 'convinced that Ornette Coleman was making a unique and valuable contribution to "tomorrow's" music because of the startling power of his playing to reach the most basic emotions' (sleeve note: *Tomorrow Is The Question*). LeRoi Jones[2] saw Coleman as 'the most exciting and influential innovator in jazz since Parker', while Henry Pleasants collected as many negative quotations as he could in order to attack Coleman for the 'singular noises he makes'[3].

In Britain, the intelligent wing of the reactionaries was represented by the articulate Alun Morgan who greeted the first Contemporary album with deep suspicion (*Jazz Monthly*, June 1959). He was quick to spot that *Jayne* used the *Out Of Nowhere* chord sequence but added that 'Coleman appears to be handicapped by his own bad fingering in places and frequently produces two simultaneous notes an octave apart'. He then posed the questions, 'Just how many discordant notes, not part of the harmony, may be fobbed off as passing notes?' and 'Is this degree of freedom desirable?'

Max Harrison and Don Heckman took a very different view. Heckman (*Jazz Monthly*, July 1960) saw no reason why 'melodic improvisation should continue to be dominated by a sequence of mechanically recurring chords'. Harrison (*Jazz Monthly*, December 1969) agreed and, although initially he thought 'Coleman's innovations too radical', he did acknowledge their high, musical quality. He began by feeling that Coleman was 'unlikely to effect a link-up with general, musical development', but these were early days and Harrison was soon to place Coleman at the forefront of the contemporary mainstream.

Fans were divided and opinion varied from sycophantic adoration to total rejection. The latter faction failed to appreciate the music's folky charm and heard only the breakdown of previously inviolable traditions. Describing sound is never easy, however, and the point could be made that, had Coleman's supporters told more about the joyfulness of his music and less about its structural freedom, they would have had more converts.

To the cursory listener, Coleman's playing in 1958 would have sounded as untutored as had that of Johnny Dodds to the Chicago and New York listeners of the early twenties. The inhabitants of those towns know little of the New Orleans' style and accepted the bland toned sound of their own players far more readily. There had to be a considerable degree of re-thinking before they could accept the great clarinettist's sweeping glissandi and his throbbing vibrato.

To talk of a human voice quality in Coleman's sound is, perhaps, too convenient, not to say even a trifle naive. Nevertheless, if the comparison is accepted as a simple analogy, it can be of some value. In Coleman's jazz the changes of texture do extend from conversational burr to gutteral exclamation. His jazz is colloquial Texas, he is not afraid to repeat a point, nor to descend momentarily to tittle-tattle. It could be claimed that his musical dialogue is deliberately catachrestic and that his malapropisms are delivered to shock the overly intellectual. More reasonable is the assumption that he is using a vernacular that comes naturally to him.

'There are some intervals' he told Nat Hentoff (sleeve note: *Something Else!*) 'that carry that human quality if you play them in the right pitch. I don't care how many intervals a person can play on an instrument: you can always reach into the human sound of voice on your horn if you're actually hearing and trying to express the warmth of a human voice'.

When considering this aspect of his playing, much was made of the fact that he used a plastic alto saxophone. It was claimed that he did so to achieve this vocalized quality and to make his sound distinctive. The truth was somewhat different. It was bought for no other reason than that he needed a replacement and could not afford a brass instrument. He reasoned 'Better a new horn than one that leaks', but added (to Gary Kramer, on sleeve note to *Change Of The Century*) that 'it began to take on my emotion. I came to like the sound and I found the flow of the music more compact (sic)'.

By this time, however, his critics were looking for any excuse to fault the newcomer. They saw the plastic horn as another vulnerable point in his armour, pointing out the instrument's shortcomings and claiming that it produced a synthetic sound. Certainly, it was a different sound but its plumminess was an aspect exploited quite brilliantly by him.

New York is Now

Perhaps the most significant thing about the Contemporary records was the fact that they brought Coleman to international attention. Of more practical importance was the fact that they attracted the attention of the Atlantic Record Company and, in the early part of 1959, Coleman was signed and immediately invited to record. This turn of events did much for his self confidence and this was reflected in his performance. Whereas his Contemporary releases had been flawed proclamations, his New York recordings represented a jazz encyclical that was to influence the course of jazz for the next twenty five years.

Eight titles were made on one day and Atlantic had captured one of the greatest of all jazz musicians working at the height of his powers. It was the first of a series of sessions that can be placed alongside the Louis Armstrong Okeh's, the Charlie Parker Dials and Savoys and the Miles Davis/John Coltrane Prestige and Columbia's as an example of jazz at its most unpredictable, its most innovatory and, inevitably, at its most influential.

On the slower items, he evoked the sadness of the natural tragedian, almost capturing the timelessly bluesy mood of the dirt road singer. It certainly did not stretch credibility too far to compare his brief and moving solo on *Lonely Woman* with the twelve majestic bars with which Johnny Dodds transformed Lovie Austin's 1926 recording of *In The Alley*. It was a performance with a similarly unforced poignancy, one that spoke of folk poet as much as it did jazz musician. Both told a story with integrity and both spurned histrionics and false embellishments.

Almost in complete contrast, the medium tempo bounce of Coleman's solo on the beautiful *Peace* had more of an affinity with the gently contoured music of swing era giants such as Johnny Hodges and Benny Carter. With Coleman's solo there was an absence of sequential organisation but the effortless symmetry of the music was very similar. Coleman was re-writing the rules and he was doing so with little regard for the sensibilities of his reactionary critics.

What became very apparent, was that, despite its radical aspects, Coleman's music was in the mainstream. His links with the past were strong, he embraced the uneven meter of the primitive blues singers, yet his solos were never distorted because of it. His approach was pragmatic, if the phrase suited it was used, he was prepared to be judged as to its appropriateness. He shared with Thelonious Monk the conviction that there were no unchangeable rules regarding timing, yet his solos progressed in a natural and pleasing manner.

There were times when Coleman actually assembled his solos in a manner that was structurally at odds with this rhythm section. He would play a series of twelve bar blues choruses over a bass and drum background that extended certain twelve bar patterns by a four bar addition. Because of the blues' essentially four, four, four breakdown it created no real tension and the listener found himself mentally compensating until the return to the status quo.

All jazzmen have clichéd phrases and Coleman was no exception. It can be argued that a brilliant improviser is a man with a huge repertoire of such 'licks' and an ability to place them in the right context and in an acceptable order. The altoist's own pet phrases told of his bebop heritage, of his blues band experience and of his formal studies and he certainly used them to good effort.

His note placing was quite brilliant and it was used in a way that suggested an intuitive, rather than a learnt skill. An important ingredient in the Coleman time mix was his frequent use of held notes. These had dramatic importance in his solos, they were deployed in a similar way to the flatulent, Lester Young 'honks', although they were occasionally delivered with a snarl more reminiscent of trumpeters Cootie Williams or Hot Lips Page. They were achieved with the octave key and embouchure arranged so as to give both notes of the octave and they can be explained as the device that had caused Alun Morgan such discomfort.

The perceptive British critic was obviously not the only observer with reservations. Atlantic Records themselves were unsure of what they could do with their controversial star. Should they believe the detractors or should they allow Coleman's own statements to speak for themselves? In the event, they took a rather strange course of action. In the August of 1959, they sponsored his attendance, together with trumpeter Don Cherry, at the School Of Jazz at Lenox, Mass., and the jazz world was presented with the absurdity of the era's outstanding, musical iconoclasts being asked to return to the basics of an earlier style.

Fortunately, it was not the abortive exercise it might have been. Coleman entered into the spirit of the thing and discussed his ideals with tutors and pupils alike. In particular, he was befriended by composer, musician and critic Gunther Schuller and together they edited the recorded music that was later issued as *The Shape Of Jazz To Come*, the Atlantic release already discussed. On the subject of Coleman (Martin Williams sleeve), Schuller says 'His musical inspiration operates in a world uncluttered by conventional chord changes, and conventional ways of blowing or fingering a saxophone.' His was 'not a surface logic, it is based on subtleties of reaction, subtleties of timing and colour that are quite new to jazz'.

Attention was again focused on his music, so much so that he was invited to bring his group into the Five Spot Cafe in New York. There he opened to a storm of critical abuse and ill considered praise and it is probably true to say that the majority of musicians and critics were, at least, suspicious of the new music. He was not without important allies, however, and pianist and composer John Lewis, remembering their San Francisco meeting, said that 'Coleman was doing the only really new thing in jazz since the innovations of Gillespie, Parker and Monk in the mid forties'. Cannonball Adderley, in a masterpiece of understatement, wrote in *Down Beat* that he was 'sure that there was a place in jazz for an innovator of this type' but, in general, the establishment was not convinced.

References were made to the 'Emperor's new clothes' and the term 'charlatan' was uttered by well known musicians around the bandstand. Ironically, several of these men had themselves suffered for their devotion to progress and they were certainly men who should have been more guarded.

On the surface, Coleman remained unmoved and his phlegmatic resolution and serious approach to his music began to win friends. It was not an overnight success story but some of the sceptics began to re-examine the man and his music, as well as to look at their own motives and prejudices.

An important factor for Coleman in the Autumn of 1959, was that he was working regularly with a stable line-up, three men who had grown musically with him and knew what was demanded by each individual composition.

Don Cherry played a pocket trumpet. His tone was small but distinctive and he had a natural feeling for the music. He made no attempt to achieve the overall *legato* feeling displayed by Coleman, yet the two men exchanged points of inspiration from each other's solos, sometimes transforming them and totally changing the mood of the selection in hand. Cherry was anti-lyrical in a way that gave the music excitement, yet there were contrapuntal passages that literally hung together solely because of him. He was less dramatic than Coleman and this tended to get him assessed merely as the altoist's alter ego. Nevertheless, the continued level of inspiration that he displayed on the Atlantic recordings was enough to discount such faint praise.

Bassist Charlie Haden was a white man in a black band. He had at his disposal a history of bass playing that stretched back at least thirty five years. In this musical environment, however, it was a history that was denied him. Immediate predecessors, such as Ray Brown, Paul Chambers and Richard Davis could be no more than spiritual influences. The rules for the instrument had changed and Haden was required to adjust the role of the bass accordingly.

He realised that he had to match the music's rhythmic licence but, more importantly, its great, melodic freedom. Coleman decreed that he 'forgot about the changes' and build for the group, at times complementing the horns and, at others, moving freely alongside them. Both things he did quite brilliantly and it was his powerfully propulsive bass line that has won over many dissenters to the Coleman cause.

Billy Higgins had matured into a natural for the quartet and, at times, he revived the Eddie Condon story in which 'even the drums played the melody'. He swung effortlessly, at times seeming almost oblivious of the tension around him, and he fed the group on a mixed diet of rhythmic orthodoxy and highly accented, free line drumming.

Had circumstances been different, however, he would not have been in the group. He was actually a protégé of Ed Blackwell and was only in the group because his mentor was unavailable at the time. Both had been part of the Los Angeles experimental team that had included Coleman, Bradford and Clay. At that time Blackwell, nine years his senior, had taught Higgins a great deal about drumming in this free jazz environment. The recordings were proof that he had responded well.

The irony of the situation was that this superb quartet, one that was turning the jazz world on its ear, actually contained two players who were realistically second choice. As good as Cherry and Higgins were, Coleman would probably have used Bradford and Blackwell as trumpeter and drummer, had he been able.

In that simple fact, lies the secret of successful, collective woodshedding. Once everyone within the group is conversant with the main aims, there can be an almost limitless permutation of sidemen playing the parent style. It was the Minton's Gang, the Miles Davis, Gil Evans, Gerry Mulligan Capitol Band and the Lennie Tristano school over again.

Atlantic Records were certainly impressed, although the controversy involving musicians such as Benny Carter, Art Farmer, Ruby Braff and Herbie Mann, began to attract a tremendous amount of interest. The point that these eminent musicians overlooked was that they were criticising Coleman for playing brilliantly in a new and, by no means, easy style. He was being castigated for being unable to follow a chord sequence, when this was what he was deliberately avoiding.

He was, in fact, exposing himself to the most testing of musical formulas. The bebopper, losing his way in mid solo, could return to the security of the chord sequence. No such escape route was available to Coleman, as statement followed statement, it had to be judged on its own individual merit. The trite phrase was cruelly exposed as such and a breakdown in continuity could threaten the whole piece.

Coleman rode these difficulties with a loose rein and used the spur of sensationalism very sparingly. He recorded again in the October of 1959 but, despite producing another outstanding record (*Change*

Of The Century) the element of critical hysteria, both pro and con, continued.

Musician-critic, Don Heckman, produced an article full of insight in *Down Beat* (9 September 1965) and used *Ramblin'*, a brilliant title from the October date, to draw attention to the fact that there might be more formality about Coleman's music than, at first, seemed to be the case. He drew attention to the restrictions that were placed on the soloists by means of the recurring rhythm section patterns and pointed out how this affected Cherry in particular.

By traditional standards, however, Coleman's jazz was informal and it was interesting to note that, when the quartet next went into the Atlantic studios in July 1960, they included in their programme, *Embraceable You*, the Gershwin standard. For the session, drummer Ed Blackwell had returned to replace Higgins but such had been the youngster's powers of assimilation, there was little rhythmic change. For his part, Coleman despatched his *test case* with aplomb although, needless to say, he saw it as nothing of the sort. The outcome was a daring piece of chromatic re-evaluation to place alongside anything by masters of the fragmented line, from trumpeter Red Allen, through saxophonist Lester Young, to pianist Thelonious Monk.

Benny Carter decided that 'from the very first note, it was miserably out of tune' and gave it two *Down Beat* stars for courage. A more realistic view might have been obtained had that gifted but reactionary player been asked to assess the 'wrong' harmonies of Monk's masterful assassinations of *Just A Gigolo* and *Sweet And Lovely* before making his deliberations. Like the pianist, Coleman had consciously re-designed the material to the exent that it became a totally new piece of music. The treatment differed from that meted out to his own compositions in that Coleman remained true to the structure of the original and did not use it merely as a starting point for free improvisation.

If this showed the way in which he treated standards, his meeting with Gunther Schuller introduced him to Third Stream music. It must be said that he was already receptive to the idea and had experimented with his own 'classical' compositions while still a teenager. For his part, the former Metropolitan Opera french horn player had, for some time, examined the cross breeding of jazz and classical music and found some strong points of contact in Coleman's personal style. The Texan had tended to regard his jazz and classical music in separate terms but Schuller felt that 'there were many parallels between the (jazz) playing of Ornette Coleman and so-called serial music, parallels which *Abstraction* tried to isolate and underscore' (sleeve note: *Jazz Abstractions*).

A concert presenting their musical collaboration was given at the Circle In The Square in New York City in May 1960 and the music recorded later that year. For Coleman it was an important step. It represented the first real example of his publicly playing music outside of the jazz field and led him toward the world of formal composition.

The concert was well received by Whitney Balliett in the *New Yorker* and by John S. Wilson in the *New York Times* and Schuller was fortunate enough to be able to assemble most of the musicians involved for a recording session seven months later. Coleman's contribution to the December 1960 sessions was of paramount importance. The resulting album was issued as *Jazz Abstractions*, and Coleman's two performances gave him the opportunity to improvise freely over a background played by the Contemporary String Quartet.

The same opportunity was presented to guitarist, Jim Hall, bassist Scott LaFaro and vibraphonist Eddie Costa, even if, in the case of Hall and Costa, very little concession was made to the spirit of the project. Both played well but neither interacted with the string quartet in any really tangible way. Ironically, the aesthetic outcome of their work was reasonably satisfying. In staying at arms length, they avoided the more violent, stylistic clashes although, in so doing, they reduced the role of the quartet to that of 'rhythm section'.

Coleman, in contrast, threw himself into the project totally. He improvised superbly but, more significantly, he heard the music in an entirely different and, one might say, intuitive manner. There were uneasy moments when the strong, rhythmic displacement he employed jarred with the strong, atonal contours of the strings. What mattered was that he chose a harmonic direction totally compatible with the Schuller parts. Here was not the jazz soloist manfully (and arrogantly) trying to lift a concert orchestra.

He had almost become part of a total ensemble concept. Unfotunately, it is 'almost' that is the significant word because, for all its points of contact, we are still left with the unpalatable fact that the outcome was still a musical hybrid. We were not faced with the naive stupidity of the 'swing the classics' mentality but there was still a feeling that Coleman's jazz element was ungrammatical, that the syntactical requirements of the string quartet made Coleman appear gauche when he was nothing of the sort.

It was an experiment that had introduced Coleman to a musical genre to which he would return, and it was music making of a high order. That it finally missed absolute success, reflects no discredit on its practitioners and perhaps only goes to support the theory that musical incest, for all its dangers, offers the best and most logical route for creative evolution.

The bassist featured on these recordings was the brilliant, young Scott LaFaro. Coleman was especially taken by his work and for several months had him in his own quartet. The effect was perhaps more significant than the period of employment would suggest because it produced a situation in which, for the first time, Coleman faced competition from within his own rhythm section.

The clash came for no other reason than that LaFaro had not balanced the two vital requirements for a bassist in the Coleman ethic of the time. Haden had almost effortlessly matched his responsibilities as harmonic signposter with that of melodic rival. LaFaro did not and, to compensate for this, he put greater emphasis on the melodic, improvisational side of his playing. For this, he was eminently well equipped. He had a phenomenal technique, a natural ear and a gift for melodic expression that stemmed from his earlier experience as a saxophonist.

His solos, whether arco or pizzicato, were a joy but he lacked concern for the overall balance of the group. There were times when Coleman's playing, over his elaborate lines, was uncharacteristically stilted but, to offset these, there were contrapuntal moments when the two men fenced like duelists and the listener became oblivious of the drummer.

Where LaFaro's melodic gifts and somewhat incontinent ensemble playing were best displayed, however, was in the legendary double quartet experiment *Free Jazz*. Now rightly acknowledged as a land mark in jazz history it was initially described as continuous, free improvisation for the eight musicians involved. It was also claimed that it was made in one take, with no splices and represented just thirty eight minutes of ad libbing.

In fact, the issued thirty eight minutes was a second take. The first, (conveniently forgotten in the euphoria of the original record release) lasted for only seventeen minutes and acted as a blue print for the finished product. More important, it confounded the argument that this was a continuous, free improvisation. Like its big brother, it retained passages for individual domination and bridged these sections with loosely structured ensemble parts.

This is not to denigrate either takes as being less than remarkable pieces of music making. The small degree of preparation used actually enhanced the performance and in no way restricted the contrapuntal interplay that took place behind each dominant individual. What was particularly impressive was the way in which the personal solo lines differed from one take to another.

The same could be said of the support figures. There were no empty riffs and, although the 'soloist' temporarily on the bridge guided the ship, he had sympathetic and often contrasting, melodic shafts fired across his bows. Coleman played superbly on both takes and he was inevitably matched by Cherry. More surprisingly, Eric Dolphy, a man sometimes accused of being out of touch with Coleman's ideals, also shone. The Californian's style was unquestionably different but he bent to this particular task with gusto. He was assertive enough to carry the rhythm section with him at one point and throughout he detached himself from the principle of sequential development.

The other comparative outsider, trumpeter Freddie Hubbard, was not so effective and, in his case, he tended to remain within the parameters he set himself. In contrast, LaFaro approached his incompatibility with far more dash. On both takes he ignored the general quiddity and used his sitar-style 'solo' section as a personal showcase, while the ensemble he used as a place to upstage Haden. In one sense, his excursion into levity could have been seen as an impertinence but, in retrospect, can be accepted as a vital, contrapuntal part in a text made up of several musical languages.

The important point was that *Free Jazz* was not quite as abstract as its contemporary observers maintained. Nevertheless, it represented the first jam session style collective attempted by the freeformer, and it did use the vernacular of the then avant garde. The sheer joy that Coleman brought to his part was enough to ensure its immortality, even if the remainder of the players took some of their inspiration and impetus from him.

One thing was certain, Coleman had grown in confidence and he had reached the stage where he invited almost any musical challenge. He had found himself in demanding and experimental situations and had mastered them. Yet he had not been heard on record playing any instrument but the alto saxophone. This was surprising in view of his earlier blues experience but this matter was put right when he played tenor throughout a 1961 session, his last for Atlantic Records. Of his decision, Coleman said 'The tenor is a rhythm instrument and the best statements negroes have made, of what their soul is, have been on tenor saxophone' (A.B. Spellman, sleeve note: *Ornette On Tenor*).

What was immediately apparent was that Coleman was as unmistakable on tenor as on alto. He translated his uniquely plummy sound to the bigger horn although, in his hands, it was not the paramour of instruments. Coleman's tenor did not woo in a gushing manner. It was forthright, was delivered with the same candour as his honest and cleanly articulated alto. Inevitably, it exhibited the greater power of the instrument but it did lack something in dynamic contrast. Coleman kept the same creative standards but was less able to create the impression of tonal extremes.

One thing that the use of tenor did highlight, however, was Coleman's ability to 'swing'. The term itself is shrouded in ambiguity and it is important to arrive at an acceptable definition before examining the matter further. One of the most simplistic was provided by Hugues Panassié. He said[15] 'Swing springs *from* regular rhythmic undulations ... the accentuating of the weak beats and sliding onto the strong beats. It is increased by the imaginative multiple accentuations of the musicians who, in sidestepping the regular rhythm ... build up the tension and increase the rhythmic impact on the listener.'

This is a reasonable way of describing what goes on 'around the metronome' and would certainly describe the way in which Coleman gave almost all of his performances a rhythmic momentum beyond actual note values. Nevertheless, opponents had already suggested that his swing was illusionary; that the real impetus came from the accentuations provided by his bassists and his drummers. This was very rarely true and never less so that on a title such as *Cross Breeding* where Coleman divided his tenor 'solo' into two parts – one with bass and drums and the other entirely alone.

There could be no doubting the validity of the rhythmic interplay that took place between the three men together but, if anything, it was the purely solo choruses that most clearly demonstrated Coleman's outstanding talent for note displacement.

Faces and Places

Shortly before the tenor session, bassist Jimmy Garrison had replaced Scott LaFaro, tragically killed in a road accident, and later Charlie Moffett had taken over the drum chair. The year 1961 also saw Coleman re-united with Bobby Bradford. Coleman had tried to persuade the trumpeter to take part in the double quartet *Free Jazz* experiment, only for Bradford to return the cash and air tickets that had been sent. By the summer of 1961, however, Bradford decided that, with his university summer session over, he would join the band. Coleman should have been delighted; he had called Bradford 'one of the best trumpet players alive' and the group were enjoying their second lengthy stay at the Five Spot. Certainly, much had improved for Coleman since his first spell at the club but this was a residency that presented problems of a different kind. In his first tenure, most of the trouble had come from the outside, from reactionary musicians and critics and from the verbal protests of the 'Coleman is anti jazz' lobby. In the second, there was some degree of internal unrest. It came to a head one evening when Garrison, normally a mild mannered man, interrupted a set at the club in front of a sell-out audience. At the time, Coleman was flabbergasted and he told A.B. Spellman[4] how the bassist had shouted 'Stop this goddam music, ain't a fucking thing happening, what do you Negroes think you're doing? You going crazy, I mean it's nothing, you know, nothing's happening, what are you doing? I mean let me have it, I know what's happening'. The music stopped and only after an embarrassed silence did the band resume playing. Coleman was naturally displeased and there is no doubt that the mood of the set was totally destroyed. Nevertheless, in retrospect, he was far more generous. He saw Garrison as a very soulful musician and one with a strong sense of his own conviction. He told Spellman that he understood, and that he could see that 'right then there was something happening with him that had a stronger meaning than what we were doing'.

This was a particularly benevolent attitude but it was consistent both with Coleman's approach to free, musical expression within his group and with his personal policy of fair shares for all. He accepted Garrison's frustration and, at least to some extent, applauded the bassist's reaction to it. Unfortunately, Coleman did not often enjoy such open hearted treatment from the non-musicians in his life. It seemed that artistic success in New York had brought him everything except money. He had made very little from the records he had made and had begun to resent the money paid to lesser talents. He found out that he had been paid less than half the sum given to Dave Brubeck to work at the same club despite attracting larger audiences.

Such discoveries led to a particularly unsettled period of his life and it was suggested that he had 'withdrawn his labour'. Some saw it as a sabbatical but, in reality, Coleman began to work rather less because he began to demand a fair price for the job. In fact, his last recording for some time came from a 1962 concert at the New York Town Hall, organised and financed by himself in an effort to beat the *system*.

That he only *broke even* is of little significance but, musically, it was an important event. With Bradford gone, Coleman used only Moffett and new bass player David Izenzon. The trio concept suited him well and he gave the audience a glimpse of the teenage Coleman by joining company with the Nappy Allen r and b trio in an item called *Blues Misused* (unissued on record). It was almost a three strata performance, with the subtle interplay of Izenzon and Moffett, superimposed on a basic blues beat, and Coleman flowing above it all with his own brand of free expression. Few people, at the time, could have realised that this backward glance at Coleman's career was also a prophetic preparation for the middle seventies.

Equally significant, was his chamber music selection, *Dedication to*

36

Poets and Writers, performed by a string quartet alone. Emotionally, it had something of the same folk music feeling that distinguished the work of Bartok but the harmonic language was culled from later styles. It certainly had no technical or syntactical link with his jazz language and made no attempt to graft on the rhythmic qualities of jazz.

He had freed himself from academic restraints and had concentrated his thoughts on the relationships between the individual voices of the quartet. Architecturally, the piece was loose but the polyphony was not undisciplined. If one could point out one basic shortcoming, it was in the music's lack of emotional range. The temper was lightly melodramatic with a tinge of sadness, and the up tempo interlude toward the close, only confirmed the thought that, at this stage, he was locked into that more pensive mood.

Apart from private and unissued recordings with Albert Ayler in 1963, Coleman was not to record again for two and a half years. He refused to lower his standards and Bradford was actually present on the occasions when appearances at the Newport Festival were turned down in 1962 and 1963 (see *Melody Maker*, 17 July 1971). The offer had been $1,500 for one afternoon but Coleman had said 'That's all right for me – now what about the rest of the band?'

It was not an attitude to make friends, nor was it one that got regular employment, but he believed in what he was doing and was determined to be nobody's *easy take*. His trio appeared only rarely in public, sometimes with Bradford, but only when it suited Coleman. Finally, the trumpeter, tired of this turn of events, returned to Texas and left a trio seemingly without work or hope.

Ironically, Izenzon and Moffett did not seek alternative jazz jobs of any significance. The bassist took work mainly in the classical field, while Moffett returned totally to his teaching career. The drummer did take some spare time jam session gigs to keep his 'chops in shape' but, ostensibly, it was as if the two men were awaiting Coleman's *second coming*.

In Coleman's case, the inactivity was equally frustrating and he took steps to put things right. He tried to open his own club and actually went as far as to purchase a property for that purpose. Unfortunately, his business naivety defeated him. The building was in a residential area, he fell foul of the licensing and zoning laws and the club was closed before it could open. He had no more luck with a publishing company that he launched at that time and he returned to his music a wiser man.

In this area, things were better. He continued to extend his studies in harmony and composition, while instrumentally he took the massive step of teaching himself to play trumpet and violin. Domestically, it was an unhappy period for Coleman himself, in the main because it marked the final breakdown of his marriage. Coleman had always spoken with charity about his wife and was full of praise for her loyalty during his troubled times. She appreciated his refusal to sell-out when financial rewards were not commensurate with the artistry and industry that went into his work. Slowly, however, she had begun to despair of reaching the crock of gold at the end of his creative rainbow. She, not surprisingly, could not understand why a man with successful records in the shops and himself the subject of international acclaim, could not earn a good living.

She felt that very little compromise was required and was disappointed when the comfort she had envisaged failed to materialise. Even his friends could not always understand his obdurate inflexibility and, although Coleman recognised his wife's reasonable needs, he found himself unable to meet them and, finally, the couple separated. Coleman was greatly affected by this breakdown of marriage and, early in 1965, he decided to go to Europe, as a chance to sort out his life.

Obviously this was not quite as simple as it appeared. He needed the money to finance the trip and, because of this, was forced to ignore his principles. Merely as a means to an end, he accepted a job at New York's Village Vanguard for less than he felt his trio were worth but he got his money and, in the event, the group's performances were almost universally acclaimed. The leader's 'new' instruments were viewed with some suspicion but Coleman again found himself in the limelight.

It was a situation that sorely tested his resolve. He was immediately invited by young American film director Conrad Rooks to make a sound track for his film *Chappaqua*. At first he demurred, as he was still determined to 'get away' and was, in any case, unsure of the wisdom of accepting a challenge outside his musical terms of reference. Finally, he was persuaded and, with arranger Joseph Tekula, tenor saxophonist Pharoah Sanders and stalwarts Izenzon and Moffett, took only three days to produce the whole performance.

The galling thing was that, after Rooks heard it, he decided against its use. He commissioned a replacement score from Indian sitarist Ravi Shankar and was alleged to have claimed that he found the Coleman work altogether too beautiful; that it would have actually been a distraction for film audiences. Since he must have known what to expect when he hired Coleman, this was a strange reaction. Whatever the truth, his decision disappointed Coleman who, after his initial reluctance, had become highly involved with the project and it was small consolation to him that Rooks decided to release the unused sound track as a record. At least, by doing so, he had allowed the general public a chance to judge it as a musical work in its own right and to see that, unlike any other piece recorded, it simultaneously presented two sides of Coleman, the jazz musician and the formal composer.

Comparing it with *Poets And Writers* was enough to establish that most, if not all, of the writing was by him. In a record review at the time (*Jazz Journal International*, September 1967), I saw 'the writing as broadly pantonal and as bridging the gulf between Coleman, the writer of formal works and Coleman the brilliantly inventive jazzman'. The suite was primarily a series of trio performances, typical of the group's normal output. The scored passages did not direct them in the thematic sense and served merely to add a sense of form to the overall work. More important, especially in the first 'movement', which was the most heavily scored, they introduced extra contrapuntal lines with strong and contrasting harmonies. They were deliberately legato and devoid of any rubato effects in the jazz sense and, set against Coleman's essentially departmentalised solo statements, created an antithetical, musical atmosphere.

In purely aesthetic terms, the contrast between Coleman's jocular, dancing alto lines and the brooding, at times almost vexacious backgrounds, was extremely effective. The film itself had its dramatic, visual spots as well as its violence, and one could have argued that such similarly dramatic music would have served its purpose well. Nevertheless, the act of Coleman gambolling along over his own occasionally turgid score parts, told us where his inspiration lay, vis-à-vis his learned skills. The somewhat studied string parts seemed to 'force' their excitement, their counterpoint was slightly mechanical, whereas the alto parts were an affirmation of his free, musical spirit. For Coleman it was a job well done but, whatever the outcome, it in no way affected his decision to change his theatre of operations.

Coleman arrived in Europe in the summer of 1965 and made London his first stop. He was welcomed with open arms by Britain's modern jazz community and shared an appartment for some time with photographer John Hopkins. Unfortunately, working was not such an easy matter. The ludicrous quota system of player-exchange, dreamed up by the British musician's union, was still in operation. This applied only to non 'classical' musicians and decreed that, unless nominated players transferred to the States, Coleman and his two colleagues could not play in the UK.

To overcome this farcical situation, Coleman had to assume his classical hat. He had to prove that he was not a jazz musician and to do so had to submit a chamber work at very short notice. The author can certainly vouch for the pressures that this caused because there were several occasions when Coleman sat through unavoidable social gatherings, still actually writing parts.

Despite the problems, the work, *Forms and Sounds*, was submitted on time and duly approved. This left British poet Mike Horovitz and his Live New Departures unit free to present Coleman and his music at Fairfield Hall, a modern concert venue in Croydon, just south of London. There was time for only one rehearsal by the Virtuoso Ensemble, a quintet of flute, oboe, clarinet, bassoon and horn, but the performance of *Forms and Sounds* was surprisingly good.

Coleman described the piece in the programme as 'a combination of diatonic and atonal intervals that creates a form out of a sound and a sound out of a form in which the five instruments blend, not by coming together, but by moving in opposing directions'. It was realised in ten movements and, like his string quartets, was rather limited in emotional and rhythmic range. Where it scored over earlier pieces was in its use of linear sound shafts that were used to react against each other. The effect, although static, was quite beautiful and perhaps gave a preview of similar sound exercises from the ECM label in the seventies.

Despite the importance of the occasion, the auditorium was far from full but those that were there were enthusiastic and they were present for only one reason. That was to hear Coleman, the jazz musician, playing with his (to them) new trio and to be introduced to his trumpet and violin playing. There was one mindless dissenter, but his raucous interjection gave the audience a superb example of Coleman's excellent and spontaneous sense of humour. In *Silence*, there were appropriately lengthy, tacit breaks and, during one of these, a barracker challenged Coleman to 'Now play *Cherokee*'. He responded immediately with a neat paraphrase of the main theme statement but, drawing no response from his 'critic', spelt it out in words of five musical syllables.

The remainder of the audience were in no mood to criticise and this did lead to an equally rapturous applause for his violin and trumpet playing. In conscience, it must be said that he was to play very much better on these instruments, most particularly on trumpet, but here was a chance to look at the inexperienced violinist and trumpeter.

A.B. Spellman[4] felt that his trumpet sounded 'curiously like Don Cherry' while 'sounding amazingly like himself (on alto)'. Obviously, such a situation is perfectly possible because both were from the same artistic milieu, originally sired by Coleman. The reality was somewhat different and musicians' reactions to his trumpet, for instance, were not always as charitable. Freddie Hubbard suggested that 'he should not play in public', and added that 'he could have done what Ornette was doing when he was five years old'[5]. Shelly Manne said that 'If Ornette wants to play more than one instrument. . . he ought to learn *how* to play more than one'. (*Down Beat*, 2 November 1967).

Obviously, his trumpet playing was 'like his alto' in a way that his formal compositions were not. It was rhythmically similar and adopted the same chromatic stance. What it did not exhibit was the same controlled method of execution. In the liner note for *An Evening With Ornette Coleman* Victor Schonfield saw his violin and trumpet playing as an 'abdication of conscious control, and a reliance on pure chance', an opinion with more to recommend it than the total put-down by musicians like Hubbard and Manne.

In fact, linking the two instruments was a valid way of evaluating them. It was so, because Coleman's violin playing represented the more radical departure, even from the relative orthodoxy (in 1965) of his alto. It took the vocabulary as far from the sighing romanticism of Ray Nance and Stephane Grappelli as it was possible to go but it was not a random exercise. A theme 'taken' by Coleman's violin was not so much rebuilt, as given a new state. It was stretched to extreme lengths for emotional impact, but was never allowed to cross the narrow line into total abstraction. One could recognise flurries used on the alto and sense that the shape of the performance had been realised in the same irregular way.

It had opened a whole new side to this remarkable musician's repertoire and it launched him on a tour of Europe that was, at least artistically, a total success. Almost immediately, he found himself with another film soundtrack commission, this time for the Belgian Living Theatre Group. The film itself, *Who's Crazy*, had been made in Belgium in 1965. It had no dialogue and was conceived to be shown with a musical background.

The one real problem that Coleman had to face was that he had not been the original choice. The producers found him on their doorstep and had decided to approach him in the hope that he could use existing material. In the event, a small amount of extra material was produced but items like *Sadness*, the opening number at Fairfield Hall, and *European Echoes*, soon to be recorded in Stockholm, proved to be the backbone of the score, recorded in 1966 in Paris.

The film itself was hardly spectacular but the trumpet and violin pieces did add a certain surrealistic charm. The most successful sound and vision synthesis came with the alto on *European Echoes* where the waltz-time theme commentated on a run through the snow. In view of the constraints involved, the outcome was reasonably satisfying and, once again, the material was released as a record.

Its appearance confirmed Coleman's complete involvement and a dirge performance on *Wedding Day* could be ranked with anything he had recorded. *Mis-used Blues*, the unissued title from the Town Hall concert, also appeared, it inspired a joyous alto outing and became the skeleton from which the later *Broadway Blues* was constructed. It was, however, the free violin rantings on other titles that were more significant, in that they offered evidence that Coleman had very rapidly come to terms with the instrument and with the possibilities for its use within his own ethic.

A bonus from the event was that an ABC television film called *David, Moffett And Ornette* (*Tempo International*, 26 June 1966) was made at the same time. It was hardly an artistic triumph but it offered sight of the trio in action, and included somewhat lightweight interviews which, at least, showed the three men in a good light.

The tour was progressing well and, if anything, it was the club dates that accomplished most in selling Coleman to an intrigued Europe. At the Golden Circle in Stockholm the trio was recorded for the first time by Blue Note, and the significance of such a move escaped the eyes of few observers. Here was the label that championed the best of the hard bop movement, presenting the accolade of a live recording date to the *enfant terrible* of the free jazz world.

An additional, but very pleasing, factor was that the actual records appeared very quickly, review copies being in the hands of the critics, within four months of the recording date. It was a chance for the committed to study the new trio in detail and, as it turned out, a let-out for the sceptics who had begun to note the tremendous influence that Coleman was beginning to have on young musicians on both sides of the Atlantic.

The trio was, in fact, an unlikely fusion of talents. David Izenzon's musical education had begun with him singing in a Pittsburgh synagogue, he had later studied bass and had worked with numerous symphony orchestras. He was, of course, yet another of a long line of white bass players that Coleman used in the early part of his career. Perhaps because of his brilliant technical skills he personified Coleman's compromise bass player in a world where he could not get the ideal one.

When asked by A.B. Spellman[4] why Jimmy Garrison had been the only black bassist used in his earlier years, Coleman had said 'I have never run into a black bass player that could keep up with my own growth in music. I haven't found a white bass player that could really keep up with that growth either, but what they could do is take the instruction, a very involved instruction, much faster'. This would certainly have been true of Izenzon although, in the looser weave of a trio, he was less restricted than had been Haden in the quartet.

Izenzon's facility on the bass was both asset and liability in the trio. His arco pitching was faultless and his articulation when playing pizzicato almost breathtaking. In view of this, it might seem to be carping to criticize his contribution to the trio. Nevertheless, there had to be a feeling that his pre-occupation with intricacy, for its own sake, did not help the altoist in his more austere and moving moments. At fast tempos, Izenzon's independent, melodic line provided a tension that stimulated Coleman to his most exciting, chromatic freedom. On the slows, this was not the case and the bassist's use of the available, harmonic licence did not always service the group's best interest.

Like the similarly gifted Scott LaFaro, Izenzon occasionally paraded his dexterity at the expense of vital, contrapuntal responsibilities. In so doing, he perhaps shone light on the problem that Coleman had outlined in his discussion with Spellman.

Charlie Moffett was an altogether different case. He started his musical life as a trumpeter in Coleman's home town of Fort Worth, Texas and played with him on that instrument while still at high school. He began his percussion studies at sixteen but, within three years, was welterweight champion of the US Navy's Pacific Fleet. He later got a BA in music and for eight years taught in Texas high schools.

With Coleman, his highly rhythmic, but not altogether complicated style, was very much at home. He was a left handed drummer and he used this contingency to good effect. His ride cymbal figures deftly filled the gaps in Coleman's essentially broken line, while his right hand completed the polyrhythmic tatoo with frequent excursions into double time. His role within the group was obviously more clearly defined than that of the bassist but his function was not purely rhythmic. Like his leader, he exhibited a fine control of dynamics. To this end, he listened with great care to both Izenzon and Coleman and, whether at a whisper or in a thunderous shout, played nothing that was not both apt and propulsive. On the rocking *Faces And Places* he took a strangely stilted solo but, in his band parts, he was the player most responsible for that piece's tremendous impetus. Coleman played beautiful alto throughout; at his most eloquently melodic on *Faces And Places* and at his most plangent on the elegiacal *Dawn*. The latter, not a blues in the orthodox sense, elicited a performance from Coleman that was steeped in an almost abject sadness. It was a slow blues in all but shape and, although a brief up tempo passage whipped aside the crapes briefly, it only served to confirm the mournfulness of what it was – a true lament.

44

Morning Song was something of a contrast and provided evidence that slow tempos did not always tempt Coleman into dirge territory. It was, in fact, as much a descriptive piece as had been dedications such as *Jayne* and *Chippie*. The listener could almost sense the countryside coming to life with the rising sun. The touch was deft and the mood was one of expectation rather than resignation. Still a young man, Coleman sounded immediately more mature. It was as if the tribulations of the recent past had brought an added depth to his already expressive style.

The whole club performance was a success and, although the muted audience response was evidence of Swedish reserve, the leader was pleased with the outcome. He was less confident about the reception he might receive on his next port of call. The French, so often European leaders in the acceptance of new jazz movements, had taken to free form rather more slowly. Nevertheless, Coleman was available and was invited to perform at the 1965 Paris Jazz Festival. Rather more surprising was the fact that he was asked to take the top of the bill spot, last on stage on the Thursday. Sonny Rollins had played a storming trio set before him, but the Coleman group acquitted themselves well.

It must be admitted that that assessment comes only second hand from a musician friend of the author. The only review to come to hand in English was in *Jazz Journal* by one-time modernist, but now long-term reactionary, Mark Gardner. In an incredible attack, Gardner (*Jazz Journal*, January 1966) said 'I still find it impossible to enjoy one of his improvisations' and 'I steadfastly refuse to accept that what Coleman is doing can be classified as jazz, because he breaks all the rules that have governed the music for sixty years.'

Apart from accepting that Coleman, by emerging in 1958, made the period of sixty years seem a trifle long as an estimate, Gardner had hit upon the truth. Yes, Coleman had changed the rules, as had Louis Armstrong and Charlie Parker: the argument was really about semantics. Jazz or not jazz? To most people, it hardly mattered. What was certain was that Rollins, the man Gardner had so justifiably praised in the set before, was a devoted Coleman admirer. He had talked at length on music with him and as early as 1962 had recorded in a style that acknowledged Coleman in its concept.

Apart from one or two other reactionaries, European critics responded positively to Coleman and in the 1966 *Melody Maker* poll,

British critics voted him Musician of the Year. The merit of such competitions is questionable but, as an acknowledgement that the most influential jazzman of 1966 was Coleman, it was acceptable enough.

In the April and May of 1966, Ornette Coleman was booked into Ronnie Scott's Club, London, for a full four-week tenancy. The Scott establishment, with New York's Village Vanguard, Blue Note and Sweet Basil's, probably amongst the most prestigeous of all clubs, was an ideal venue. Popular with performers, its atmosphere was ideal for the trio. They had time to unpack, settle down and concentrate on their music.

Seven visits to the club in one month were a salutary experience for this writer. They showed to what degree Coleman improvised each solo, even to what extent he took new directions within it. With no chord sequence as a crutch, Coleman was sustaining a level of free improvisation that placed enormous pressure on him. He was thinking further ahead than his more traditionally-minded peers and he was leaving himself marooned on only the rarest occasion.

What surprised many observers was that he was playing a normal brass saxophone. The effect on his tone was not great and was probably only noticeable in the lower register, where his soft, plummy sound had a slightly harder grain. His higher notes seemed unaffected and he achieved the same harsh, astringent sound that came over as one of the most beautiful and moving in jazz. In any case, he assured me that the plastic horn was undergoing repairs on the Continent and that he had no intention of permanently switching to the more orthodox instrument.

Finally, this was not the case and the Scott audience were literally seeing the change-over point from plastic to brass. Unfortunately, there was one section of that audience who were party to history repeating itself. Just as one sector of the establishment musicians had been on hand to ridicule at the Five Spot Café, so they did at Scotts. Well-known players were present on more than one occasion to pass noisy comment and, it was no comfort to note that, at least two of them later became part of the British free form movement.

The important point for those who wanted to hear, was that Coleman was improvising on tunes like *Dee Dee*, *Sadness* and *Wedding Day* in a totally different way, night after night and, in so doing, was playing some of the most brilliant jazz ever heard in the club. The themes still set the tone of each piece no matter how short and simple they were. At times, the most rudimentary tune promoted the most cleverly realised and involved solo but, throughout, Coleman maintained an umbilical link with the mother theme. It was jazz of a very high order.

In the summer of 1966, the trio returned home to America. The tour had been tiring, artistically successful and not the financial disaster that might have been expected. It had exposed Coleman to an adoring, European public, and had perhaps tested his cynicism in respect of ill-informed sycophants. Admittedly, European ears had been prepared by records and by the more perceptive American critics but their response had generally been extremely enthusiastic. Coleman returned home, his confidence renewed.

The reality of New York was not quite so reassuring but it was not as bad as before. Blue Note wanted more records and Coleman was offered club dates in and out of the city. It was, in fact, his first Blue Note date on American soil that once again took him into the centre of controversy.

His son Ornette Denardo was now ten years old and living in Los Angeles with his mother. For his sixth birthday present, Coleman had bought for him a set of drums and this had really fired the youngster's interest in music. Later, he had taken lessons and by the age of nine was a proficient (musical) reader. Before going to Europe, Coleman had played alongside his son and he had promised that, when he returned, *they would record together*.

The record date took place four days before Denardo returned to school in California and there were four rehearsals. Izenzon had been reluctant to play without Moffett, and Coleman returned to his old colleague Charlie Haden. The title track, *The Empty Foxhole*, had been written earlier in Los Angeles and the remaining five were put together while the youngster was in New York for the summer recess.

The record's appearance stirred up a critical hornets nest. Coleman was accused of blind nepotism and of again trying to put people on. He had perhaps just won over the conservatives, and there he was again throwing down the gauntlet. Shelly Manne described it as 'unadulterated shit' (*Down Beat*, 2 November 1967) and went on to point out that the 'kid would probably turn out to be a good carpenter'. On the magazine's rating scale, he gave it minus

47

five stars. In contrast, Cannonball Adderley gave Coleman himself five stars but the record only three. He distrusted the rhythm section and said (*Down Beat*, 2 November 1967) 'I don't like what those people were doing. . . what they played was like interruptions to me'.

Reactions were mixed, but most agreed that Coleman was playing well and that his son was a promising but unspectacular drummer. The more generous said that it was remarkable playing *for a ten-year old* while the less charitable said 'so what?'.

This observer tended to side with the latter. There was an underlying rhythmic strength and enthusiasm in the drumming but beats were missed and tempos were inconsistent. Yet, inexplicably, it suited the music and in a brilliant article (*Jazz Monthly*, July 1967) Jack Cooke proposed the theory that the backing, with Haden steadfast and Denardo wayward, was just what Coleman wanted. He postulated the idea that the use of the child was compatible with the altoist's idea of playing *without memory*.

Who better than a naive ten-year old, with nothing to unlearn, to produce fresh responses and new outlooks to an existing formula. This Denardo undoubtedly did even if his playing was, at one moment inchoate, at another inspired. His worse drumming occured on an up tempo item called *Freeway Express* where he was both wayward and rather stiff. His best was against Coleman's floating, almost ghostly, line on *Faithful* where he played highly personal fill-ins, complementing both bass and alto perfectly. Finally, it would have to be conceded that the music would have been better had Coleman used a more mature player such as Moffett or Blackwell.

Coleman summed up the experience (*Down Beat*, 2 November 1967) by saying 'I felt the joy of playing with someone who hadn't had to care if the music business or musicians or critics would help or destroy his desire to express himself honestly'. Although it was no less significant that his natural reserve prompted him to add that he was 'very sad to have to sell his son's talent without his knowing the life this type of existence might make for him'.

One aspect of the record that was not acknowledged to any great extent was that, for the first time, Coleman devoted complete numbers to his trumpet and violin. *The Empty Foxhole* itself was a short piece that Coleman played straight. His trumpet tone remained thin and he employed the same declamatory and rather 'old time' start to each phrase. At the time, it was suggested that it might have presaged a move toward the kind of musical economy that had occurred in the careers of similarly evolving players. Louis Armstrong and Coleman Hawkins are two that come readily to mind.

A more protracted look at Coleman's trumpet was presented early in 1967 when he was invited to play on a recording date with Jackie McLean. Surprisingly, the New Yorker asked him to play trumpet on every track as it would 'best complement each other'. In one way, this was a disappointment because it would have been quite an experience to have heard the two altoists locked in 'battle'. McLean, however, had a healthy respect for his guest's trumpet playing and told Nat Hentoff (sleeve note: *New And Old Gospel - Jackie McLean Quintet*) that 'he was amazed how far Ornette had gone on that horn in three years'. He was not about 'to compare Ornette technically to anybody. . . only to point out how much he played and to the fact that what he played was entirely him'.

The reality fell somewhat short of those lofty sentiments. Coleman was more at home on his own compositions and he took comfort during his solo on *Old Gospel* from the rolling, baptist rock laid down by pianist Lamont Johnson, bassist Scott Holt and drummer Billy Higgins. At less accommodating tempos, he did not hit notes with the required fulsomeness and there was almost an apologetic air in his delivery.

Certainly the aura of certainty, taken for granted in his alto work, was missing. The faintly tentative mood of the trumpet gave up different charms, however, and it gave his playing an appealing, almost vulnerable quality. In a Mutt Carey or a Bunk Johnson it would have been acceptable.

By his own standards, it was some distance from his finest work but the listener could almost sense that working one whole date on trumpet was better for his chops than the brief horn flirtation that might occur in other circumstances. It raised the interesting point. Just how much time was Coleman giving himself to prepare? Certainly in concert and, one suspects, on record dates, he did not play the trumpet long enough to get his lip in shape. An established horn man is never too happy to play just one or two numbers but to do so immediately after playing alto is not to be recommended.

This observer has watched Benny Carter play alternate tunes on

49

trumpet and alto throughout the night at New York's Sweet Basil's Club, but has also watched major multi-instrumentalists, such as Ira Sullivan and Joe McPhee, struggle in similar circumstance. Coleman was perhaps demanding just too much of himself.

Certainly in the early months of 1967, Coleman was concerning himself with the trumpet. After returning to America, he wrote trumpet interludes to add to his European written *Forms And Sounds*. He did this purely to allow him access to his own piece and he included it in a concert given at the Village Theatre in New York in the March of that year. Of the work he was now rather more forthcoming and, in his own liner notes he referred 'to "improvise reading" where an instrument had the possibility of changing the piece by a change of register. For example, the flute and the bassoon could both play a C in the treble clef and be three octaves apart – in other words, when the piece had a performance the instruments could change the register of their passages, cause the music to sound different and thus change the form each time it was played'.

On the night, Coleman duly joined the Philadelphia Woodwind Quintet. The players in the quintet had obviously had more time to rehearse than had the Virtuoso Quintet in London. The result was a more disciplined performance but one that put into even more stark relief the playing of the principal. In fact, he played impressively and made no attempt to transform the work into jazz or, for that matter, 'third stream music' in the accepted sense. His playing, however, was that of a jazz musician and it lent a rather unrealistic feeling to the overall recital.

For the pure jazz part of the programme, Coleman used a quartet. Haden had rejoined his mentor and the group boasted two bassists. Blue Note recorded the proceedings but, as yet, have not released the music on record.

The bass men in tandem were an important part of Coleman's group philosophy in the ensuing months and were in the quartet that was billed to play at London's Albert Hall in February 1968. Again, he ran foul of the Musician's Union exchange system and, on this occasion, had even less time to write a non-dance, non-jazz piece. His credentials were in better shape than on the early occasion, however, because, just before setting out for London, he had been awarded a Guggenheim Fellowship. The foundation had commissioned a work for the thirty-five piece orchestra of the

Philadelphia Symphony and it was scheduled for performance at the Lincoln Centre in New York later in the year.

This did not overly impress the British musician's union, however, and Coleman set about the task of writing his 'classical' composition. It was called *Emotion Modulation* and it appeared in time for the London date. This time there was not the smokescreen of classical musicians and it actually took up the entire first half of the concert. It was a continuous work and it comprised several movements; formal divisions were avoided and each theme provided a basis for extended improvisation. Izenzon explained in an interview with this writer, that rehearsals had made no attempt to prepare the final product in exact detail. Instead, the musicians gradually evolved and developed each thematic unit until Coleman's skeletal structure had the flesh added.

Both bass players made the trip but the drum seat had again become the property of Ed Blackwell. Coleman treated the audience to alto, trumpet and violin and, for good measure, played *Buddha Blues* on musette (or Shenai, as he called it). The unexpected guest was Japanese composer, singer and part-time film director Yoko Ono. She had had two operas, *Grapefruit In The World Of Park* and *Strawberries And Violin*, both premiered at Carnegie Hall and had toured extensively as a singer with John Cage.

Her contribution on *Emotion Modulation* was brief but shattering. Her vocal was not the phonetic sound exercise that might have been expected. It was, in fact, the sound of a woman making sexual love. The group provided no contrived, erotic effects and Yoko Ono merely stood on that very lonely stage, moaning with an ecstasy that was frightening in its realism. On a purely aesthetic level, the actual sounds she made dovetailed beautifully with Coleman's trumpet and Blackwell's economical and static drum figures and fully justified the title of the work.

Whether it could be called jazz, again hardly mattered. What was certain was that, after the singer had left the stage, the audience were treated to the brand of jazz normally associated with Coleman. Perhaps the most challenging selection was a string trio called *Three Wise Men And A Sage*. It found Coleman on violin and had the bassists switching roles, with Haden taking the arco parts and Izenzon ranging freely with the pizzicato. Coleman's folkish fury sounded crude but it had an ineluctable vitality. The sheer emotional projection compensated for the limitations in technique and it showed just how near he had brought the violin to the turbulent excitement of his alto.

In order to get a work permit, he had spent many hours convincing the authorities that he was not a jazz musician. In the Albert Hall, he spent little more than two proving he was one of the greatest.

Friends and Neighbours

The first real change in musical policy since 1962 occurred when Coleman returned to America. He was joined by tenor saxophonist Dewey Redman, another Fort Worth expatriate and a man who had reason to believe that arranging pioneer and saxophonist Don Redman was his uncle. He had been at school with Coleman and, although a useful musician, had tended to concentrate on a more academic career. The change came in 1960 when he moved to San Francisco and, for the next seven years, devoted far more time to his music.

While there, he established quite a reputation, one that stood him in good stead when he moved to New York and was re-united with his schoolmate. His arrival meant that, for the first time since the departure of Cherry, Coleman had a permanent horn partner and he was one who was to stay with the band for almost six years.

In 1968, Redman was already a very good musician and it was inevitable that he would have had a profound effect on the group. Coleman now had someone with whom to share the solo responsibilities in a way that drummers or even bassists could not. Predictably, he did not exploit the contrapuntal opportunities thus presented, although a brief passage on *Round Trip* showed how ideally suited to each other they could be in this aspect of group playing.

In other respects there was some stylistic distance between the two men. Redman's big tone and more legato approach was almost of another era. It had more in common with Archie Shepp's brand of aggressive romanticism, yet it produced a contrast that worked in practice.

To add further colour to his tone, Redman had devised a method of singing through the horn to produce an effect not dissimilar to that achieved by Roland Kirk on flute. Because of the characteristics of the horn, this was obviously more difficult but Redman made it an integral part of his style. On its own, it would have been little more than a distinguishing feature; one smacking rather of the glib gimmick. Where it became a serious, musical tool was when he chose to extend the tonal range of his music, by means other than the use of the false upper register.

Despite the considerable gulf between their basic musical directions, there was no stylistic antagonism. Redman's free flowing phrases and emotional blood letting was the perfect foil for his leader's more tense, almost astringent style, although the presence of drummer Elvin Jones, must have helped the young tenor when he first joined. He certainly had more in common with the Detroit giant than did Coleman.

It is not difficult, however, to explain the brevity of Jones' stay with the band. Up to this date, the part that Coleman's drummers, Blackwell, Higgins and Moffett had played was clearly defined. Coleman had always required straight ahead swing, with perhaps an emphasis on a ringing, high cymbal and with rhythmic fragmentation kept to a minimum. Such a policy was obviously alien to Jones and in the operational dichotomy that occurred, we find both the reason for the experiment and the reason for its only limited success.

Jones' brilliantly accented drumming had served John Coltrane perfectly. Its climax points were never obvious and his tremendous swing was cloaked in a shroud of subtle complexity. His approach encouraged a sense of linear detachment from the horns and, as such, it suited Redman. Coleman did not play badly with Jones but, for their partnership to have worked on a more permanent basis, there would have had to be changes on both sides. Jones would certainly have had to simplify his line, while Coleman would have probably looked at an increase in rhythmic intensity.

In the event, they parted company, although the return of a slightly older Ornette Denardo in the following year did nothing to enhance the group. He had improved in certain departments but his method of accentuation remained tense and his cymbal work had, if anything, gone backward. Coleman had just joined fellow modernists like Shepp, Coltrane and Pharoah Sanders on Impulse and that label was pursuing a healthy, contemporary jazz policy.

Unfortunately, Coleman's first release was hardly a triumph. Denardo's unsympathetic drumming was quite a stumbling block and on *New York* one is tempted to suggest that the leader ushered the group into a faster tempo just to get his son together. On the credit side, Haden was now back in the combo on a permanent basis and it was he that provided the elasticity in the rhythmic backgrounds. He had had a health problem during the sixties but, by 1969, was fit and playing better than ever. It could be suggested that, because of the shortcomings of the drummer, he was forced to broaden his own scope, both in his solo projection and in the authority of his solo work.

There was a latent power about his playing at this period. It was like a controlled thrust but it gave the feeling that he could move up a gear if an increase of impetus was appropriate. Coleman certainly reacted more to him than to his son, although observers were not slow to point out that a quartet is a rather public place for a passenger to hide.

In the late sixties and very early seventies, Coleman worked in public less regularly. He won several international polls as leading altoist, however, and could have been very good box office material. Unfortunately, he was continuing his one man vendetta against club owners and bookers. He felt that most of them made capital from the fact that jazzmen are notoriously determined to play on almost any terms. He was determined not so to do and again resorted to performing only when the circumstances and the venue were right for him.

Don Cherry returned for a concert at the Loeb Student Centre at New York University in 1969, and together they gave a performance to confirm that they remained musical compatriates. There were even odd appearances by the 'original quartet' in the manner of the ODJB or M.J.Q. revivals although, on a more serious level, Cherry was the added voice to the quartet with Redman. They were not re-united for long, however, because Cherry had been increasingly attached to Europe and it was not long before he again left. By 1971, he had married his artist wife, Moki, and had settled in Sweden.

Fortunately, it was at this time that Coleman found a place of his own in which to play. Number 131 Prince Street was in the SoHo section of Manhattan and he appropriately dubbed it the Artist House. Originally he took the second and third floors of the building but later agreed to take over the first (ground) floor for his own work. He had the area soundproofed and began an open-handed policy of encouragement to the arts. He placed no restrictions on race, class or creed and the doors were open to musicians and dancers alike. These people would frequently leave gifts or items of their own creation but few were actually charged.

It was a policy that fostered good feeling and the musical soirées and happenings at the house became quite legendary. Ironically, the only recorded evidence was provided by a record issued without Coleman's authorisation, but it did document the degree of audience participation that was encouraged. Friends and neighbours sang along with musicians and felt at liberty to shout encouragement in a very uninhibited way.

Unfortunately, as so often happens in such circumstances, Coleman's philanthropic attitude made some people suspicious and, in 1974, he was victim of a plot to remove him from the premises. He had papers that he thought gave him the tenancy but several people moved in and said they had bought the building. Coleman was adamant that they had bought nothing from him but told this writer that 'one of their wives told me that they were going to pick a way to get me out because they didn't want any minorities there and *they* were scared'.

At first Coleman was fazed because he thought they were artists and that they would all cohabit amenably. The truth was that they had real estate aspirations and did not want minorities living in that area. They went to court claiming that they had bought the building and a series of legal wrangles began. Coleman became disenchanted with the fight and within the year had left the Artist House for good.

During his period at the house, Coleman continued to set himself new challenges. For a recording date by Alice Coltrane he did the transcription of the string arrangements and, although Chicagoan Leroy Jenkins was among the four violinists that played them, their connection with jazz was scant. The mood of the record, the ancillary instruments used and the titles themselves took the music into the quasi-Asian field. The string parts were perhaps closer to his non-jazz writing for woodwinds or string ensembles but there was the uneasy feeling that it came too near to the music of a film soundtrack. Alice Coltrane's keyboard hand can be strongly felt and, in comparison with the quartets, they must be considered unambitious.

In the open arena Coleman was better employed. The Newport Jazz Festival had recovered from the earlier riots and, after a restful 1970, had been given back the fourth of July, 1971. In the heat of a glorious Saturday afternoon, Coleman walked out in a watermelon-red suit and beguiled the audience with a superb set. Like Charles Mingus before him, he earned and received a rapturous ovation and was rated as star of the show by more than one commentator.

Ironically, criticism came from his back when Mingus told Whitney Balliett that 'he felt sorry about jazz. The truth had been lost in the music. All the different styles and factions had gone to war with each other and it hasn't done any good. *Take Ornette Coleman*'.[5] The bassist had gone on to sing half a chorus of *Body And Soul* in a loud, off-key voice and to declare that 'That's all he does. . . just push a melody out of line here and there. Trouble is, he can't play it straight.'

Coleman again had reason to feel betrayed, and again by an iconoclast who might have been expected to understand the loneliness of the artistic, long distance runner. It was probably small consolation that Joachim Berendt, reporting on the 1971 Berlin Jazz Days, heard him as 'simply making beautiful music,' or that Ron Brown (*Jazz Journal*) reported that, in the London concert of that year, 'Coleman poured out a torrent of melodic ideas, while wrenching hearts along the way'. The author was also present on that night and can vouch for the fact that Coleman was in brilliant shape and that he did much more than 'push a melody out of line'.

In 1971, Bobby Bradford finally got to record with Coleman. The near misses of the past, the telegrams at the time of the Double Quartet recording, were all behind them and, finally, a studio opportunity presented itself while the trumpeter was in the band. The band of the period also included a temporarily returned Cherry and, for the recording session (*Science Fiction*) they were joined by vocalist Asha Puthli, trumpeters Gerard Schwarg and Carmon Fornarotto as well as Redman, Haden, Blackwell and Higgins. Bradford was the sole trumpet only on *Law Years, The Jungle Is A*

57

Skyscraper and *School Work* (issued later on *Broken Shadows*) but his playing provided an opportunity to compare the effect that two such different trumpeters had on the group.

Unlike Cherry, whose brittle and fragmented inspiration always sounded spontaneous, Bradford was a lyrical player, whose lines flowed in a seemingly well prepared manner. As such, they fitted the superb bounce of this rhythm section quite perfectly and, even in the turmoil of *The Jungle Is A Skyscraper*, his spitting arpeggios took the music along a more legato path and perhaps suggested that there might have been greater emphasis on fluency, had he been the quintet's permanent horn man.

Skies of America

Ornette Coleman had written his first classical composition by the age of nineteen and, even during the fifties, he had interspersed his jazz work with periods devoted to 'serious' music. The New York String Orchestra had performed his work in New York Town Hall in 1959 and, in 1964, he appeared before 13,000 people with the San Francisco symphony.

In 1962, Gunther Schuller dedicated two classical pieces to him, and between 1964 and 1966 Coleman included classical pieces in programmes throughout Europe and America. As mentioned earlier, 1967 saw his Guggenheim award and it also saw the recording of his most successful non-jazz works so far. Two string quartets were recorded by the Chamber Symphony of Philadelphia Quartet and they were despatched with effortless expertise. *Space Flight* was a light hearted piece but the poignant *Saints And Soldiers* was of the highest quality. Coleman claimed that it was inspired by his visits to churches in Rome in 1965. There he had found urns containing the remains of saints and soldiers, and thought it incredible that persons of such opposite beliefs – each in his own way attempting to influence the world – could end up in exactly the same place.

Musically, they were unorthodox quartets and hearing them performed by the Philadelphian quartet or seeing their scores, would give no clue that they were the work of a jazz musician. This was not a view held by Coleman himself, however, and in his sleeve notes he claimed that 'the themes that the quartet played as the opening were the kind of writing I had learned from playing the trumpet, sax and violin'.

In aesthetic terms, *Saints And Soldiers* was a very moving work. All four melodic lines were clearly defined and they were both gentle and strong. The counterpoint was never cluttered, the emotions never tense but the four musicians involved were encouraged to interact in a way that was self inspirational. This contrapuntal dovetailing was important but each part had a status of its own. To claim that each could have been a solo in its own right, would have been to overstate the case but there was a melodic richness in them that tempted such a suggestion.

Good as these had been, it was 1972 that saw the performance of a Coleman work that rates as his greatest non-jazz triumph. *Skies Of America* was recorded in London with the London Symphony Orchestra under conductor David Measham. There were two full-scale rehearsals and the actual recording session took nine hours. All of the compositions and orchestrations were by Coleman and in his music he expressed the hope that future Americans would care about the American Indians 'whose skies gave so much'. Photographs taken in the studio by Valerie Wilmer (*Jazz Journal* June 1972) gave the impression of calm activity and amiable co-operation – the quality of the music upheld that theory.

On the album sleeve note Coleman described *Skies Of America* 'as a collection of compositions with the orchestration for a symphony orchestra and based on a theory book called *The Harmolodic Theory*, using melody, harmony and the instrumentation of movement of forms. . . . The writing was applied to harmolodic modulation, meaning that it modulated in range without changing keys.' It was a continuation of the theory outlined by Coleman at the time of his *Forms And Sounds* performance, using his own trumpet. For the first time he was actually classifying the music as *harmolodic modulation* and going on to explain that 'the movements were written free of key and making use of the total collective blending of transposed and non-transposed instruments, using the same intervals'.

The astute Gary Giddins described it as 'the finest symphonic writing to come out of jazz'[7] and the work did earn Coleman a standing ovation from the eighty five musicians involved. In reality, it moved from the unashamedly descriptive to the almost esoteric abstract. By keeping the voicings in very high parts, he got good, dynamic contrasts and achieved his objective of getting a musical dichotomy that spoke of earth and sky, and of day and night.

For him it was almost a commentary on what the skies overlooked. *Place In Space* took the listener on a swirling journey through dangerous space junk into the area of Sun Ra's intergalactic music. Otherwise sights were set at more mundane targets and musical shots were fired at the entire history of America. Doomy movements were not ignored but much was made of the hurly burly of birthdays and funerals and the good life in general.

Coleman managed a section for dancers that has been used by contemporary dance groups but he also took an introspective stance for *All Of My Life*, a reflective piece that featured no alto but came near to imitating its use. Perhaps this effect was heightened by the remarkably free tympany that calibrated the formal sound shapes in a pleasingly irregular manner.

More than any other section, it posed the question; would it have been a more proper course of action to have stayed out of the recording as a performer? The parts taken by his own ad-lib alto could easily have been written for someone else and so avoided the disruptive appearance of his fiery, but not altogether compatible, horn. On the *The Men Who Live In The White House* he avoided the problem by making it a totally solo performance but the only title on which he managed to make his beautiful alto playing belong was against the congested backdrop of *The Artist In America*. His closing coda was the ultimate in impudence but the whole piece gave as firm a confirmation of what Coleman was hearing inside his own head as anything he had produced up to that date.

Following another European tour toward the end of 1972, Coleman went to Africa. While in Morocco, he came into contact with the Master Musicians of Joujouka in the Rif Mountains. The meeting took place during the Festival of Boujelaud and it resulted in Coleman recording with the locals. He told Richard Williams (*Melody Maker*, 17 March 1973) 'I saw thirty of them playing non-tempered instruments in their own intonation, in unison.' They changed tempos, intensities and rhythm and used drums, purpose built to establish their pitch and timbric value.

The altoist not only played with the Master Musicians; he also worked with local singing groups and indeed whole villages, although such 'happenings' would not seem to be ideal material for recording. The intuitive aspect of the Master Musicians' music struck a responsive chord in Coleman – it was playing 'without memory' in a different context.

Likewise, the Master Musicians, with no concept of European pitch, found a degree of common ground with Coleman. Their own individual octave became a usable foundation and on *Midnight Sunrise* a compromise was reached. By jazz standards the rhythm was complicated but rather static and it was as if it was used as punctuation rather than as a stimulant.

Superficially, it seemed that neither Coleman nor the Master Musicians seemed even remotely interested in what the other was playing yet, somehow, their unconscious efforts found compatibility. There was a strange, almost accommodating quality in the 'unisons' of the Moroccans which, if not exactly the organ chords of a swing band, became a welcoming cushion for Coleman's animated and wailing alto.

For Coleman it was an act of atavism and Valerie Wilmer[8] was quick to note that it was as if 'Coleman had gone back to what jazz had originally been about. . . individuals not worrying about the written note in order to blend with it'. The music they made together was untidy, but it did have the beauty of undisciplined folk music.

Unfortunately, the problems that beset his regular band in 1973 were not musical but medical. Drummer and good friend Ed Blackwell became unwell and moved in with Coleman for a time. Thinking that he was suffering from ordinary back trouble, they visited a chiropractor only to find that it was more serious. Almost immediately Blackwell lost the use of both kidneys and required constant dialysis machine treatment. The alternative, and obviously the best permanent solution, was an operation but, even at the time, this involved a cost of around $50,000. Fortunately, friends both within and outside the music world rallied around this popular man and the surgery was completed.

Coleman had been extremely supportive and this was typical of the man. He valued his friendships and was loyal to those around him. His hardness in the negotiation of appearance money, recording contracts and other commercial factors did not affect his social world and, if anything, turned him toward those he loved rather more.

The intimacy and availability of the Artist's House was valuable to all concerned in the middle seventies but Coleman did not get into the recording studio for a session of his own for over three years. There was a French session with Claude Nougaro in 1975 and a guest appearance for Charlie Haden in the March of 1976 but it was not until December 1976 that Coleman's name was again used to front an album.

Important changes had been going on, however, and 1975 had seen the introduction into his group of a rock influenced guitarist, an electric bassist and a congo player. The changes in the music were inevitably radical and for the first time Coleman referred to his non-symphonic music as harmolodic.

It was a case of role reversal. No longer could he claim that it was the lessons learnt as a practising jazzman that dictated the stylistic direction of his formal compositions and his chamber music performances. Here was the harmolodic theory applied to his regular band, and he had chosen the men to do the job.

The 24th Newport Jazz Festival of 1977 saw Coleman's first real New York concert since 1973 but it was done in style. The evening was his totally, and he was presented in a highly imaginative manner. The first section teamed him with former colleagues, Cherry, Redman, Izenzon, Blackwell and Higgins. To these were added bassist Buster Williams and the then current guitarist James 'Blood' Ulmer, and this excellent line-up was presented with a programme of new Coleman compositions.

Williams and Izenzon adopted the roles of LaFaro and Haden in the manner of the Double Quartet venture, while the drummers played with the same superb cohesion as they had in December 1960. The use of new material, the change in horn players and, most especially, the presence of Ulmer, ensured that the resulting music was very different from that of sixteen years earlier. One could not say that stylistic links with the past had been broken, however, but with Cherry, Redman and the leader in such fine shape there was no danger of it becoming a nostalgia trip.

In contrast, the second set was very different and it gave the New York concert goers their first taste of the essentially electric group that had been born in the preceeding year. It was as if Blood Ulmer's mid concert interlude had been included to be the mental ferry that carried the audience from the established Coleman tradition to the new sound of his group Prime Time.

The Prime Time line-up had been established a year earlier, and it included guitarists Bern Nix and Charles Ellerbee, bassist Rudy MacDaniel and drummers Ronald Shannon Jackson and Denardo Coleman. Dan Morgenstern described the music (*Jazz Journal International* August 1977) as a failed attempt at jazz soul fusion and, on the evidence of a 1976 date in Paris (*Dancing In Your Head*) he was probably reporting with characteristic sensitivity. The French recording had certainly suggested that the group's riff based style could founder as the background became muddled.

The vital point that this overlooked, however, was that now the harmolodic theory was in the working place. Its arrival was complicated for new listeners because of the rhythmic stance that accompanied it. Gone was the backbone throb of Haden's bass and the superbly light shuffling rhythms of a Blackwell. In its place was a cross pattern of rhythmic accents, pitched not only at constant levels of intensity but also given to changes of volume and individual emphasis.

The one distinct constant from the past was the leader himself. The style and make-up of his own solos had not changed to any appreciable extent. The effortless flow of freely associated ideas still dominated his method of delivery. Criticisms of the rhythm section, however, were not without foundation. The drummers tended to respond to each other rather than to Coleman while MacDaniel never questioned the musical route as had Haden and Izenzon. He was a pulse player because Coleman wanted a pulse player. His responsibilities did not take him on personal journeys of discovery and he was a map reader rather than an explorer.

In one important way, it was history repeating itself. Prime Time's backgrounds, for all of their higher aspirations, were closely related to those of the contemporary, heavy rock groups. Swing, in the traditional sense, was not an objective and one was tempted to suggest that its complexity failed to disguise its somewhat static movement.

It was, in many ways, like listening to Louis Armstrong playing with the 1930 Les Hite Orchestra. There, Armstrong, the inspirational liberator of the jazz soloist, had played above the turgid band parts almost as if oblivious of them. At times his detachment was so extreme that his own melodic line moved behind the pulse – almost a bar adrift! It was as if he regarded only what he had to say as

Ornette Coleman in Copenhagen, 1987. Photo: Jan Persson.

above: (l to r) *David Izenzon, Ornette Coleman, Charlie Haden and Charles Moffett at the Village Theatre, New York, 1967.* Photo: Raymond Ross Photography.

below: *Scott LaFaro, with Ornette Coleman on plastic alto, at the Monterey Jazz Festival, 1960.* Photo: Ray Avery.

above: *Billy Higgins, Ornette Coleman and Dewey Redman at Carroll's Rehearsal Studios, New York, 1977.* Photo: Raymond Ross Photography.

below: *Jamaaladeen Tacuma, Ornette Coleman, Charles Ellerbee and Bern Nix at the Hollywood Bowl, Los Angeles, 1982.* Photo: Ray Avery.

above: *Ornette Denardo Coleman, Ornette Coleman and Sabir Kamal at the City College, New York, 1984.* Photo: Claudia Thompson.

above: *Charles Moffett at the Actual 81 Music Festival, London, 1981.* Photo: Jak Kilby.

above: *Ed Blackwell at the Philharmonic Hall, Berlin, 1986.*
Photo: W. Patrick Hinely, Work/Play.

below: *Don Cherry and Ornette Coleman at the Delphi Theatre, Berlin, 1987.*
Photo: W. Patrick Hinely, Work/Play.

above: (l to r) *Ornette Denardo Coleman, Pat Metheny, Ornette Coleman, Jack DeJohnette and Charlie Haden at the Song X Concert, New York Town Hall, May 1986.* Photo: Claudia Thompson.

below: *Ornette Coleman and Bern Nix at the Jazz Club Montmartre, Copenhagen, 1987.* Photo: Jan Persson.

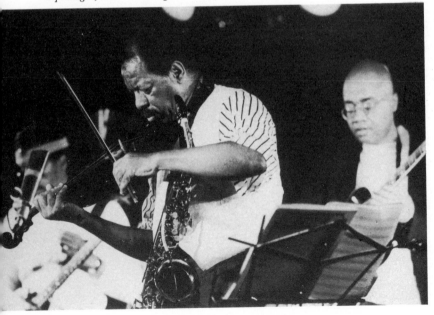

above: *Billy Higgins and Ornette Coleman at the Delphi Theatre, Berlin, 1987.*
Photo: W. Patrick Hinely, Work/Play.

below: *Old and New Dreams performing at the Hammersmith and Fulham
Jazz Festival, London, 1980:* (l to r) Don Cherry, Charlie Haden, Dewey
Redman and Ed Blackwell. Photo: Jak Kilby.

Ornette Coleman in concert at the Town & Country Club, London, 1987.
Photo: Peter Symes.

being important. The parallel with Coleman's earliest Prime Time efforts was dangerously close.

The harmolodic altoist was certainly 'free to modulate in range without changing keys' but he did not deploy his troops in the more ambitious manner of the Miles Davis rock groups. The members of the rhythm section remained just that, and rarely played a major organic part in the music's *thematic* progress. This was further born out by *Body Meta*, another 1976 Paris session dominated entirely by Coleman's own torrential improvisations but similarly short in overall integration. In fact, it is something of a measure of the Texan's skill that his superb alto on *Voice Poetry* and *Macho Woman* seems almost dissociated from the general rhythm clutter.

In complete contrast, his 1977 duo album with Charlie Haden presented two voices of equal aesthetic value. Coleman played mainly tenor and, by the very nature of the instrument, shouldered the bulk of the solo responsibilities. Nevertheless, the rapport between the two men was uncanny with the unpredictable Haden as happy as a producer of apposite countermelodies as he was as the suggester of alternative, melodic paths. Together, they moved from the bounce of *Soapsuds* to the groaning dirge of *Sex Spy* in a way that reasserted all of the 1959/60 Atlantic values.

For Prime Time, however, it was early days and the duo sessions was inevitably a one-off. Familiarity with the harmolodic principles was beginning to breed improvement in the touring group, although Coleman never denied his problems in the group's formative years. His reaction to the problems set by his free form quartet were totally different and they had inevitably led him to different conclusions. 'When I was forming Prime Time,' he told Art Lange (*Down Beat*, June 1986) 'the one thing that bothered me was that, in the past, I only played music using two horns and a bass and drums, and I wasn't doing it (to the best of my ability) because I was given other things to do. But then James Ulmer came to my house one day and studied with me, and started playing a line on the guitar, and I found out that, not only does a guitar sound like a full orchestra, but when you play a melody on guitar. . . it sounds like it's moving the melody to another place. This is the way I hear the saxophone. I don't ever hear the saxophone in a key, or, if I'm playing an idea or a melody, I never hear that idea or melody on the saxophone – I only hear it because someone had made those

65

melodies sound that way. I take those same notes and *play a totally different melody*'.

Prime Time offered him two guitars against which to respond and it took his music into another challenging field. If his free form band had asked him to 'play without memory', Prime Time demanded that he respond to a constantly changing array of musical stimulants. By the slightest hint, either guitarist could redirect a Coleman apparently in full flight, and the outcome was usually exhilarating. To make this even more of a challenge, Coleman had chosen two vastly different guitarists. Nix, with his precise phrase shapes, was more of a jazzman, while Ellerbee took his fuzzed chords unashamedly into funk territory.

Coleman made use of the contrast but neither the media nor the audience were fully convinced. Perhaps to encourage the attendance of the Coleman faithful, the 1978 Northsea Festival press release billed Prime Time as the Ornette Coleman Quintet. In the event, several hundred of the audience at The Hague walked out, as if to suggest that frankness regarding the performance would have been preferable. Certainly, Britain's Bracknell Festival, later that year, made no such mistake. The *sextet* was billed as Prime Time and, although this writer was only present at the latter event, it would not be unreasonable to suggest that the music heard at both was similar.

At Bracknell, there was only a limited walkout. The Coleman supporters were inevitably loyal but it was a good concert. The group displayed the expected rhythmic limitations but they were limitations with a purpose and they were consistent with the leader's changed approach to collective group playing. In fact, there was a suggestion that Jackson and son Denardo were beginning to include other group members in their previously personal dialogues.

Of Human Feelings

Whatever the musical output or financial rewards enjoyed by the Prime Time band, it did not please all of Coleman's followers. His name began to appear less advantageously in the polls conducted by jazz magazines and, as the American jazz world began to adopt a more conservative stance, he found himself, not for the first time, something of an outsider.

Coleman had always cared little for poll results but his intractability with bookers, club owners, festival organisers and record companies remained a stick with which he beat himself. He had appointed pop specialist Sid Bernstein as manager but still turned down work if he felt he was being exploited.

In 1979, he recorded the album, *Of Human Feelings*, for the Antilles wing of Island Records and it was destined to be his last for some time. Jamaaladeen Tacuma (formally Rudy MacDaniel) was on bass and Calvin Weston had joined Denardo in the drum team. As a record, it made a statement about Prime Time's musical policy and somehow it seemed to imply that the group was satisfied with a suspiciously cosy niche. It could be called *free form funk*, *harmolodic fusion* or whatever, but a clearer pattern of performance was emerging. The noted contrast between the two guitarists had become something of a central issue in the musical policy and it was as if two parts of the band had begun to polarize.

It was as if Coleman was translating the concept of the famous double quartet of *Free Jazz* to the needs of funk jazz. Coleman remained in control of the melody line, while Tacuma vacillated between the supporting two strata beneath. One comprised a 'melody' support team of guitar and drums, while the other became a totally committed rhythm team, also of guitar and drums. The interaction was constant and, just as Coleman could take directional hints, there were times when it was he who changed tonalities, with the others modulating as required.

At its best, it presented *What Is The Name Of That Song?*, a track that suggested that Coleman was at home in an atmosphere of busy rock rhythms or *Jump Street*, where there was a greater creative input from the guitars. *Air Ship*, however, was a trivial disco performance, bogged down by its own danceability and with no real attempt at improvisation. Yet, for all its potential commerciality, Prime Time's music made no impact on the American hit parade.

Steve Lake suggested (*The Wire*, September 1985) that 'the 1984 disco-fied version of *Dancing In Your Head* that appeared on Jamaaladeen Tacuma's *Renaissance Man* offered a tantalising glimpse into how Ornette might sound if he opted more directly for the funk market'. *Of Human Feelings* offered only a funk/jazz compromise and, as such, satisfied nobody.

Although the Antilles date was to be his last commercial release for six years, Prime Time was working regularly on both sides of the Atlantic. Coleman, the anti-social dresser of the late fifties had long since become more clothes conscious. The cool dude image presented on his return to jazz in the mid sixties had given way to the extravagantly coloured suits of the seventies. With Prime Time he went further and became unashamedly *show biz*.

His outrageous neon suits became a trade mark and the entire group dressed with an awareness of audience reaction. It hardly taxes credibility to suggest that this flamboyance was part of an overall policy and consistent with an easing of attitudes to make him more approachable. It was an accessibility that extended not only to his music but also to his treatment of the media and his own musical contemporaries.

In 1980, plaques bearing the name of musicians were implanted into the sidewalk on New York's 52nd Street. Years earlier it would have been the type of event that Coleman would have treated to the full weight of his apathy. This was no longer the case. A good natured Coleman attended the ceremony and pictures by Lee Jeske (*Jazz Journal International*) show him talking enthusiastically with Sarah Vaughan and Roy Eldridge.

This unruffled friendliness became more his public image and was especially evident when he dealt with friends and journalists during his European tours in the early eighties. This generosity of spirit extended to his reaction to Old And New Dreams, an outstanding group formed in 1976 and built along the lines of the original Coleman Quartet. It included Don Cherry, Charlie Haden and Ed Blackwell but had Dewey Redman in the saxophone chair.

The common view was that Old And New Dreams was a copy of the original quartet; that they played many of their mentor's compositions and that they set out merely to produce a recreation of the style. In fact, there was virtually no direct plagiarism. If anything, the commitment was more all embracing and it would be more accurate to see the group as the embodiment of the Coleman quartet spirit. They certainly captured the old élan and they brought to Coleman compositions new inspirational directions, albeit within the parameters of the parent method.

In Cherry, Haden and Redman the group had three vastly different composers, all conversant with Coleman the tunesmith, and each able to bring to the style a change of accent, a different, rhythmic emphasis or a highly personal backward glance at the boppish roots of the music. Titles such as Haden's *Chairman Mao* offered a suitably mock-oriental theme, Redman's *Old And New Dreams* and *Orbit Of La-Ba* exposed a special brand of exoticism, while Cherry's *Mopti* introduced a primitive element of a rather unfamiliar kind.

Coleman's tunes such as *Handwoven, New Dream* and *Open And Close* had never been issued on record under his name, although the aficionado may well find at least one of these strains more than a little recognisable. It would be more productive to observe the way in which original performances differed from the remakes. How the short but agonisingly beautiful *Lonely Woman* became a more extended piece. How Cherry, denied any real say on that Atlantic recording, dominated the Dream's version with a trumpet solo to rival the gut wrenching emotion of Coleman's superb 1959 effort. How the brilliantly contrapuntal opening of the 1969 Impulse label quintet version of *Broken Shadows* is simplified into a unison statement with arco bass support.

Such adjustments could be considered as fine tuning but, in effect, the listener became increasingly aware of the Old And New Dreams' determination to copy nothing; preferring instead to match the empirical Coleman ideal. Coleman regarded their exploits with generous enthusiasm but one could not deny that, in terms of stylistic inspiration, the band was performing in a style that had been deserted by its inspirational leader and that was now twenty years old.

In Coleman's book, this was unquestionably music of the past and he had moved on. He neither recognised nor cared about aesthetic comparisons and remained devoted to Prime Time and the harmolodic principles. This was born out by his long-awaited return to the business of making records. Appropriately, it took place in his home town of Fort Worth and was a live set played during the 1985 opening of Caravan Of Dreams, the new performing arts complex in the city. The musical programme also included the world premier of the *complete Skies Of America* symphony, as well as the premier presentation of Coleman's string quartet, *Prime Design/Time Design*.

On Caravan Of Dreams Productions' first record, however, it was Prime Time that was heard. With Sabir Kamal in place of Weston, the band played six Coleman originals, although it seemed careful to avoid being too profound. *Sex Spy*, the beautiful dirge that had proved so inspirational in the Haden duets, was inappropriately taken at a bouncing medium tempo, while *City Living* had an almost contrived joviality. Only on *See-Thru* did he project real emotionalism and it was as if he had decided that Prime Time should provide the 'light relief' in a programme including classical pieces.

Fortunately, it was not this attitude that led him to his 1985 recording date with Pat Metheny. It was a project that made sense and was a logical extension of his relationship with Blood Ulmer and the playing of Prime Time. The guitar could be 'the orchestra' and, in having Metheny as the player, it went one better. Here was a musician who was already a Coleman devotee and one who had always included a number of the altoist's tunes in his repertoire.

For him it was something very special and he told Art Lange (*Down Beat*, June 1986) that to describe the partnership as 'the high point of my experience as a musician would be an incredible understatement'. Originally it came about because Haden had seen the opportunities that it could offer and the bassist had decided to help in its organisation. He also played bass on the sessions and adopted the role of captain of the rhythm section.

The outcome was a total success. Coleman played superbly; his alto solo on *Mob Job* was a model of gentle lyricism, he took *Endangered Species* with a power thrust that created his own 'sheets of sound', while on *Video Games* he took the kind of romping solo that confirmed his reputation as one of jazz's greatest swingers. Perhaps, significantly, the highlight of the project was the delightful *Song X Duo*, an all too brief contrapuntal interlude for Coleman and Metheny, with both producing sparkling ideas that could dovetail quite naturally. It was a performance to compare with the Haden duets and it again confirmed that the challenge of the duo situation elicited maximum response from Coleman.

Coleman and Prime Time had been in Europe in the summer of 1986 but the tour had been blighted by the old malaise. Son Denardo had taken on the duties of band manager but, together with his father, had conspired to disagree with French bookers over terms of payment and performance and, without completing a tour that had been scheduled to include a British concert, the band returned to America.

Almost as if to compensate, Coleman did appear in London in 1987. Two houses at London's cavernous Town & Country Club were packed and the Prime Time band treated the audiences to a unique mixture of Texas blues, free form jazz and harmolodic funk. They exploited the two drum, two bass and two guitar situation and the leader presented himself in 'prime' condition. The performances were very much as before; Coleman dominated from the front, he coasted when required and his alto took melodic directions that kept the audience firmly on the front of their seats.

His violin was reserved for the encore but he frequently took his trumpet into chromatic areas that made his music chillingly dramatic. In the past, it had been the bassists that had provided the assured route. In 1987 it was the fierce, rock based drumming of son Denardo and Calvin Weston that provided the extra dimension; the busy clatter that suited alto, violin and trumpet alike.

There was, however, a subtle change of emphasis. Coleman's role in the earliest Prime Time performances had been indisputably that of leader and melody maker. In the 1987 edition of the group his stance was perhaps less dogmatic. Melody maker he firmly remained, but there were areas of the music where he accepted added rhythmic responsibilities and melody line and pulse began to

71

come together. In no way did he aspire to become an approximate imitation of a rhythm instrument nor to be a replacement for one. It would certainly be misleading for the listener to focus on rhythm as the reigning element but it was evident that melody was gradually becoming subsumed within the total rhythmic structure.

It was not an act of status reduction but it took his music some considerable aesthetic distance from the quartets of the late fifties. An opportunity to put the extent of this gulf into perspective came at the 1987 Newport Festival in New York City. Coleman slightly altered the performance formula of the 1977 event and presented his current group alongside a recreation of the earlier quartet's using originals like Don Cherry, Charlie Haden and Billy Higgins.

No recordings of the event have appeared to date (1988) but an album issued in 1987 offered a very reasonable representation of what the audience heard on that night. *In All Languages* was made up of studio recordings, all of the compositions were by Coleman and none had appeared on record before. Seven, however, were given interpretations by both groups and this gave the unique opportunity for a true comparison of style change; present day performances given by groups which, in theory, belonged thirty years apart.

Perhaps significantly, no qualitative superiority emerged but it rapidly became evident that there were stylistic adjustments necessary if Coleman was to function with his old brilliance in the quartet. This he did, producing contrapuntal passages and highly creative solos to show that the changes could be made quite effortlessly. His task was easier because of the superbly buoyant contribution by Haden and Higgins and, although Cherry seemed somehow diffident, this hardly affected him at all.

It rapidly became apparent that certain themes suited one group more than the other. *Feet Music*, a theme reminiscent of Sonny Rollins' *Blessing In Disguise*, drew a dancing, light-footed tenor solo from the quartet, while the leader's alto with Prime Time accepted a slower gait, using double time as a colouration. This was typical of the different forms that Coleman's solos took in the two groups, although on *Latin Genetics* they were similar in outline. Elsewhere they were dissimilar in design and, at times, even in tempo. The Prime Time's *Cloning* offered an illustration of Coleman accepting responsibility for part of the music's rhythmic progress, while *Mothers Of The Veil* elicited a good response from the quartet and a masterful one by their successors. On the Prime's version, Coleman played authoritative alto, dramatic if less technically assured trumpet but it was the entire sextet that scored with the tight knit cohesion they achieved.

The whole album had made a nonsense of historical perspective, almost as if thirty years had been distorted by a strange time warp. It again confirmed that it was futile to talk of progress or of the culmination of earlier ideas. Talking to this writer at a reception following the London concerts, Coleman stressed his forward looking approach. He added that it was Prime Time that offered the genuine status report on the Coleman career. It had been set in a style that Coleman had built up like an empirical pyramid, using all the stages that came before. The jazz world's response to the resulting conglomerate style has been consistently reserved. Whereas Coleman, the free form pioneer, had exerted enormous influence on the next generation of jazzmen, Prime Time has virtually no following outside its own immediate circle. With the inspirational presence of Coleman, the band's music is never going to be a musical backwater but, for all its potential, it must be conceded that Coleman has played with greater creativity in other company.

He has always spurned the opinions of academics and, like his sternest critic, Miles Davis, now seeks to reach a wider audience. Like the trumpeter, he has still only succeeded in part, alienating his more reactionary, jazz followers with rock rhythms and presenting music somewhat too esoteric for the pop market. To his peers, this does not seem to matter. As a great jazz musician, they judge him at the instant of creation, whatever the style or setting, and only rarely is he found wanting.

Coleman's best musical moments are amongst the most significant and inspired in all jazz history. There is a body of recorded work to confirm his position, with Charlie Parker, as the greatest of all altoists and to draw attention to his status as a composer, arranger and innovator of the first order.

Cross Breeding

Coleman's influence on the jazz world has been immense. It was the Atlantic recordings, however, that first placed him at the start of countless learning curves. Through them Coleman offered players on every instrument the inspiration to express their own personal feelings away from the framework of a set, harmonic sequence. It was not so much that he gave them a style to be copied slavishly, but rather that he opened the door to musical free speech.

The influence was all pervading but, for certain saxophonists, Coleman's method offered a blue print for performance. In meeting his style head-on, these musicians were perhaps embracing a different type of discipline. But, if it was a discipline, it did offer a sure way of breaking with the entrenched teachings of music school and with the traditions of bebop.

In the case of certain second generation free formers, the initial link with Coleman's own playing method was very strong. Byron Allen's 1964 debut album included an original called *Decision For The Cole-Man* but it was his playing on titles such as *Time Is Past* that best illustrated his debt to his mentor. It was couched in the Texan's vernacular and significantly pursued the same relaxed lyricism. The early work of men such as Marshall Allen, Henry Threadgill, Noah Howard, Jemeel Moondoc, Trevor Watts and Oliver Lake was, in itself, highly varied but, like that of Byron Allen, it came unmistakeably from the same source and could be seen as belonging to the direct Coleman 'line'.

The saxophonists of the New York Contemporary Five borrowed

in a more oblique manner. They used several Coleman compositions as starting points for their free solos but there was little incidence of phrase copying. Tenor saxophonist Archie Shepp was a wild player but he was also an effusive romantic and he rarely organised his solos in the Coleman manner. His conversancy with swing era stylists like Ben Webster and the pre-free form modernists like Sonny Rollins encouraged him to lay his solos more consciously on the beat and to employ longer lines than the older man. Altoist John Tchicai, in contrast, was the Lee Konitz to Coleman's Charlie Parker. His mood was one of understatement, space was an important component in the make-up of his solo line, and his arhythmic concept took him, at times, dangerously near to a static state. Nevertheless, the NYCF's book was peppered with Coleman tunes and their arrangements were delivered in the manner of the composer.

The scope of Coleman's influence was certainly startling but it was not always as a direct result of contact with his earliest recordings. He was actually involved in his trumpet and violin studies when he first met Marion Brown in New York during the early sixties. Coleman was very helpful to the young Georgian and, judging by Brown's first records under his own name, it was the Atlantic epics that originally inspired him. It now seems likely that it was later aspects of his friend's career that had set him on his own path to discovery. He was always to play in a more convoluted way than Coleman even if the principle of motivic improvisation was the same.

There were some musicians for whom the impact of Coleman's jazz was especially cataclysmic. It turned their world around but, in the process, succeeded in setting them off in search of a personally acceptable development of free jazz almost at once. One such man was Roscoe Mitchell, a Chicagoan originally raised on the music of Louis Armstrong and Billie Holiday but turned on his head by Coleman records while serving in the US Army in Germany.

Mitchell had rapidly embraced the free style and, on his first session as a leader, had included a tune called *Ornette*. He pointed out, however, that his profound admiration for Coleman had, by then, already stopped short of unthinking idolatry and that his course of self discovery had begun. His stylistic credentials, established within the tonal compass and harmonic freedom suggested by Coleman, had already added a spatial awareness and idiosyncratic turn of phrase to herald his departure from the Fort Worth well spring. It was a journey that took him to the halcyon days of the Art Ensemble Of Chicago.

For a man such as Anthony Braxton, it was different. He came to Coleman via Roscoe Mitchell, a colleague in Chicago. He had the analytical mind of a chess master and was, at first, resistant to the intuitive genius of the Texan. His conversion was none the less total, however, and his initial reserve could be said to have accounted for the personal way in which he came to terms with it.

Braxton was a man of parts; his improvisations could be made up of loosely, swinging phrases, blessed with a buoyant, dancing quality. Conversely, they could be built in structured sound slabs that, for all their architectural perfection, were practically immobile. Ironically, it was the latter that told us more about Braxton's situation vis à vis Coleman and, in the process, told us much about Coleman himself.

Using a musical language that Coleman had literally taught himself, Braxton had arrived at a solo design that was artfully well organised and, because of his method of delivery, transparently so. The patterns in Coleman's own performances had always been far less obvious but, judged through the bell of a protégé's saxophone, the finely-tuned degree of formal awareness suggested by Don Heckman (*Down Beat*, 9 September 1965) becomes apparent even to the most reactionary of his critics.

Not all aspects of the Coleman school's evolutionary process were as easily diagnosed and, as the third generation of devotees appeared, it was not always clear that the influence was at first hand. In the case of Jane Ira Bloom and Tim Berne, one could not help but feel that the message had been diluted by at least one interim phase. Yet, with men such as Steve Coleman, John Purcell and Eric Persons, the feeling was that the inspiration was direct. To confound such a theory, the young Coleman (no relation) lists Von Freeman and Bunky Green as his mentors and this despite the fact that, in certain musical situations he came very close to the pure Coleman style.

The Ornette Coleman influence on instruments other than the saxophone has been no less dramatic. His intimate, musical involvement with trumpeters Don Cherry and Bobby Bradford excludes them from being considered as disciples in the purest sense. Nevertheless, it was through them that the free gospel reached the likes of Bill Dixon, Alan Shorter, Don Ayler, Earl Cross, Lester Bowie, Baikida Carroll, Leo Smith, Herb Robertson and latterly Olu Dara. There was also a case of the teacher being taught as Coleman turned to the trumpet himself in the sixties using the brass adaption of his saxophone style.

Despite their vastly different responses to Coleman's music, trombonists Roswell Rudd and Grachan Moncur III both tailored it to the needs of their seemingly less fluent instrument. They were quick to realise, however, that the deliberate humanisation that Coleman brought to his saxophone sound could be transferred with equal drama to a slide instrument. They also managed to capture much of the altoist's free flowing flexibility and, in so doing, became the couriers able to pass on the message to the likes of Steve Turre, Ray Anderson and Craig Harris in the seventies and eighties.

John Carter and Perry Robinson unlocked the mysteries of the Coleman music box for the clarinettists that came after, while for the flautists it was left to two very different stylists to present the instrument's translation of the Coleman dialect. Prince Lasha had gone to school with the master and, in his earliest recordings, did little more than plagiarize his style. In contrast, James Newton, who emerged at a later date, heard, tasted and adapted Coleman's music to the unique needs of the flute.

Perhaps due to the all enveloping presence of Cecil Taylor, Coleman exerted little influence on pianists. His groups had rarely used them and, when he wanted greater harmonic stability later in his career, it was to the guitar that he turned. Guitarists were not similarly impressed. Derek Bailey and Fred Frith embraced the spirit of the freedom cause but it was left to the wild, bluesy tonality of Sonny Sharrock to come closest to the folky Coleman method. Sharrock shared the altoist's admiration for blues primitives like Blind Willie Johnson and, although he himself listed Coleman as one of his prime inspirations, it was the rock practitioners who attracted most attention in the world of latter day jazz guitarists.

In view of the tremendous impact that Coleman made on jazz, it was surprising that he had similarly scant influence on his predecessors. Both Louis Armstrong and Charlie Parker had attracted the ear of older men and, in the years following their arrival, there had been something of a scramble as musicians tried to 'catch up'. No such rush followed Coleman's appearance on the scene. For the most part, this was probably because most of the older players found his musical motives undesirable although, in some cases it was because they found the improvisational demands unattainable.

Amongst the exceptions, however, there were two players of considerable evolutionary importance in their own right. Their attempts to play the 'new music' met with very different results. This hardly mattered; the point was that they had grasped the important implications of the melodic latitude it offered. Sonny Rollins brought the full might of his instrumental mastery to bear and many of his live performances came startlingly near to the free form ideal. Predictably, his most successful recording, the 1962 *Our Man In Jazz* was made on location and, for a period of his life, Rollins fully accepted the Coleman ethic and played quite beautifully within it.

In contrast, Jackie McLean was less successful. It was as if he had grafted Colemanesque phrases onto a melodic line reluctant to part company with its thematic base. His considerable jazz know-how made the outcome superficially acceptable but, too often, this gifted player felt the need to limp back to the sheltered accommodation of the harmonic structure that he might be using.

Certainly, Coleman had re-written the rules and it was perhaps asking too much to expect brilliant establishment players to desert their natural style indefinitely. The new musical statute book had more obvious appeal for those who came after. It was for players who took Coleman's tonality for granted because it had flowed into the jazz mainstream more than thirty years earlier.

Strangely enough, Coleman's violin playing kept its own distance from the parent style and, because of this, attracted few followers. It had been his alto work that had inspired Leroy Jenkins, the finest of all free violinists, and through him the younger Billy Bang. All that Coleman's violin style had done, was to encourage everyone on the instrument to regard inspirational ecstasy as a natural form of communication.

That was a word that came to be very dear to Coleman and it was his ability to communicate that was at the heart of his appeal to other musicians. His own playing remains that of a master but he has also taught a generation of jazzmen the 'new way'. It is no exaggeration to say that he changed the language of jazz for most instruments.

Bibliography

1   *Reflections* by Marion Brown (Juergen A. Schmitt)
2   *Black Music* by LeRoi Jones (MacGibbon & Kee)
3   *Serious Music – And All That Jazz* by Henry Pleasants (Gollancz)
4   *Four Lives In The Bebop Business* by A. B. Spellman (MacGibbon & Kee)
5   *Encyclopedia Of Jazz In The Seventies* by Leonard Feather and Ira Gitler (Quartet)
6   *Such Sweet Thunder* by Whitney Balliett (Macdonald)
7   *Riding On A Blue Note* by Gary Giddins (Oxford University Press)
8   *As Serious As Your Life* by Valerie Wilmer (Allison & Busby)
9   *Free Jazz* by Ekkehard Jost (Universal Edition)
10 *The Jazz Book* by Joachim Berendt (Paladin)
11 *The Illustrated Encyclopedia Of Jazz* by Brian Case/Stan Britt (Salamander)
12 *Black Nationalism And The Revolution in Music* by Frank Kofsky (Pathfinder)
13 *The Freedom Principle* by John Litweiler (Morrow)
14 *Jazz In The Movies* by David Meeker (Talisman)
15 *Dictionary Of Jazz* by Hugues Panassié and Madeleine Gautier (Cassell)

Films and TV Features

1963   *O.K. End Here* (USA) directed by Robert Frank
A short film that looks at a woman, played by Susan Graham
Mingus, and her relationship with her man. Music by Ornette
Coleman.

1965   *Who's Crazy?* (USA) directed by Allan Zion and Tom White.
Filmed in Belgium, it offers a more than eighty-minute look
at improvisations by the Living Theatre Company of New
York. Music on soundtrack produced by Ornette Coleman
after the event and dubbed on.

1966   *David, Moffett And Ornette* (USA)
An ABC television film made at the same time as the *Who's
Crazy?* score recording. It included somewhat superficial
interviews but also featured the trio in action.

1967   *Population Explosion* (Canada) directed by Pierre Hébert.
The above trio play a soundtrack for a very brief animated
cartoon about international injustice.

1969   *Chappaqua* (USA) directed by Conrad Rooks.
Coleman has a non-speaking role in a film about Western
society poisoned by its own drugs. Coleman also wrote the
original score but this was ultimately rejected.

1981   *Box Office* (USA) directed by Josef Bogdanovich.
A feature film with a Coleman score.

Selected Discography

I have based my selections on recordings mentioned in the text and on those generally available at the time of going to press. All the recordings listed here have been issued in the USA except where noted.

The following abbreviations have been used: (as) alto sax; (b) bass; (bcl) bass clarinet; (cl) clarinet; (d) drums; (elb) electric bass; (elg) electric guitar; (Eu) Europe; (flu) flute; (g) guitar; (J) Japan; (LA) Los Angeles; (NYC) New York City; (p) piano; (per) percussion; (tp) trumpet; (ts) tenor sax; (vbs) vibraphone; (vcl) vocal; (vln) violin.

TONY MIDDLETON, *London, August 1988*

SOMETHING ELSE! THE MUSIC OF ORNETTE COLEMAN
Don Cherry (tp); Ornette Coleman (as); Walter Norris (p); Don Payne (b); Billy Higgins (d). *LA, February 10, 1958*
INVISIBLE/ THE BLESSING/ JAYNE

Don Cherry (tp); Ornette Coleman (as); Walter Norris (p); Don Payne (b); Billy Higgins (d). *LA, February 22, 1958*
CHIPPIE/ THE DISGUISE/ ANGEL VOICE

Don Cherry (tp); Ornette Coleman (as); Walter Norris (p); Don Payne (b); Billy Higgins (d). *LA, March 24, 1958*
ALPHA/ WHEN WILL THE BLUES LEAVE?/ THE SPHINX

Contemporary S7551

COLEMAN CLASSICS
Don Cherry (tp); Ornette Coleman (as); Paul Bley (p); Charlie Haden (b); Billy
Higgins (d).   *Hillcrest Club LA, October, 1958*
WHEN WILL THE BLUES LEAVE?/ CROSSROADS/ RAMBLIN'/ HOW DEEP IS THE OCEAN?
                                                Improvising artists 37.38.52
Note: other titles on 37.38.52 are Paul Bley.

TOMORROW IS THE QUESTION
Don Cherry (tp); Ornette Coleman (as); Red Mitchell (b); Shelly Manne (d).
                                                LA, January 16, 1959
TURNAROUND/ ENDLESS/ LORRAINE

Don Cherry (tp); Ornette Coleman (as); Percy Heath (b); Shelly Manne (d).
                                                LA, March 9/10, 1959
TEARS INSIDE/ TOMORROW IS THE QUESTION/ COMPASSION/ GIGGIN'/ REJOICING/ MIND AND
TIME
                    Contemporary S7569, Boplicity Contemporary (Eu) COP 002

THE SHAPE OF JAZZ TO COME
Don Cherry (pocket tp); Ornette Coleman (as); Charlie Haden (b); Billy Higgins (d).
                                                NYC, May 22, 1959
FOCUS ON SANITY/ PEACE/ LONELY WOMAN/ EVENTUALLY

Don Cherry (pocket tp); Ornette Coleman (as); Charlie Haden (b); Billy Higgins (d).
                                                NYC, October 8, 1959
CONGENIALITY/ CHRONOLOGY

                                                Atlantic SD1317

CHANGE OF THE CENTURY
Don Cherry (pocket tp); Ornette Coleman (as); Charlie Haden (b); Billy Higgins (d).
                                                NYC, October 8, 1959
THE FACE OF THE BASS/ BIRD FOOD/ UNA MUY BONITA/ CHANGE OF THE CENTURY

Don Cherry (pocket tp); Ornette Coleman (as); Charlie Haden (b); Billy Higgins (d).
                                                NYC, October 9, 1959
FORERUNNER/ FREE/ RAMBLIN'

                                                Atlantic SD1327

THIS IS OUR MUSIC
Don Cherry (pocket tp); Ornette Coleman (as); Charlie Haden (b); Ed Blackwell (d).
                                                NYC, July 19, 1960
BLUES CONNOTATION/ KALEIDOSCOPE

Don Cherry (pocket tp); Ornette Coleman (as); Charlie Haden (b); Ed Blackwell (d).
                                                NYC, July 26, 1960
EMBRACEABLE YOU/ HUMPTY DUMPTY

Don Cherry (pocket tp); Ornette Coleman (as); Charlie Haden (b); Ed Blackwell (d).
                                                NYC, August 2, 1960
BEAUTY IS A RARE THING/ POISE/ FOLK TALE

                                                Atlantic SD1353

FREE JAZZ .

Don Cherry (pocket tp); Freddie Hubbard (tp); Ornette Coleman (as); Eric Dolphy (bcl); Scott LaFaro, Charlie Haden (b); Ed Blackwell, Billy Higgins (d).

NYC, December 21, 1960

FREE JAZZ part 1/ FREE JAZZ part 2

Atlantic SD1364

THE ART OF THE IMPROVISERS

Don Cherry (pocket tp); Ornette Coleman (as); Charlie Haden (b); Ed Blackwell (d).

NYC, October 9, 1959

A CIRCLE WITH A HOLE IN THE MIDDLE

Don Cherry (pocket tp); Ornette Coleman (as); Charlie Haden (b); Billy Higgins (d).

NYC, May 22, 1959

JUST FOR YOU

Don Cherry (pocket tp); Ornette Coleman (as); Charlie Haden (b); Ed Blackwell (d).

NYC, July 26, 1960

THE FIFTH OF BEETHOVEN/ MOON INHABITANTS/ THE LEGEND OF BEBOP

Don Cherry (pocket tp); Ornette Coleman (as); Scott LaFaro (b); Ed Blackwell (d).

NYC, January 31, 1961

CHECK UP

Don Cherry (pocket tp); Ornette Coleman (ts); Jimmy Garrison (b); Ed Blackwell (d).

NYC, March 27, 1961

HARLEM'S MANHATTAN

Atlantic SD1572

ORNETTE ON TENOR

Don Cherry (pocket tp); Ornette Coleman (ts); Jimmy Garrison (b); Ed Blackwell (d).

NYC, March 22, 1961

EOS

Don Cherry (pocket tp); Ornette Coleman (ts); Jimmy Garrison (b); Ed Blackwell (d).

NYC, March 27, 1961

ENFANT/ ECARS/ CROSS BREEDING/ MAPA

Atlantic SD1394

TWINS

Don Cherry (pocket tp); Ornette Coleman (as); Charlie Haden (b); Billy Higgins (d)

NYC, May 22, 1959

MONK AND THE NUN

Don Cherry (pocket tp); Ornette Coleman (as); Charlie Haden (b); Billy Higgins (d)

NYC, October 8, 1959

UNA MUY BONITA

Don Cherry (pocket tp); Ornette Coleman (as); Charlie Haden (b); Ed Blackwell (d)
NYC, July 19, 1960

LITTLE SYMPHONY

Don Cherry (pocket tp); Ornette Coleman (as); Charlie Haden (b); Billy Higgins (d)
NYC, July 26, 1960

JOY OF A TOY

Don Cherry (pocket tp); Freddie Hubbard (tp); Ornette Coleman (as); Eric Dolphy (bcl); Scott LaFaro, Charlie Haden (b); Ed Blackwell, Billy Higgins (d).
NYC, December 21, 1960

FIRST TAKE

Don Cherry (pocket tp); Ornette Coleman (as); Scott LaFaro (b); Ed Blackwell (d).
NYC, January 31, 1961

CHECK UP/ THE ALCHEMY OF SCOTT LAFARO

Atlantic SD1588

TO WHOM KEEPS A RECORD
Don Cherry (pocket tp); Ornette Coleman (as); Charlie Haden (b); Billy Higgins (d).
NYC, October 9, 1959

THE FACE OF THE BASS

Don Cherry (pocket tp); Ornette Coleman (as); Charlie Haden (b); Ed Blackwell (d).
NYC, July 26, 1960

BRINGS GOODNESS/ TO US/ ALL/ SOME OTHER/ MOTIVE FOR ITS USE

Atlantic (J) P10085A

'ORNETTE'
Don Cherry (pocket tp); Ornette Coleman (as); Scott LaFaro (b); Ed Blackwell (d).
NYC, January 31, 1961

W.R.U./ T&T/ C&D/ R.P.D.D.

Atlantic SD1394, Jazzlore 29

AT TOWN HALL 1962
Ornette Coleman (tp, as, vln); David Izenzon (b); Charles Moffett (d).
NYC, December 21, 1962

THE ARK/ DOUGHNUT/ SADNESS

Ornette Coleman (tp, as, vln); David Izenzon (b); Charles Moffett (d); Selwart Clarke, Nathan Goldstein (vln); Julien Barber (viola); Kermit Moore (cello).
DEDICATION TO POETS AND WRITERS

ESP 1006

AN EVENING WITH ORNETTE COLEMAN
Ornette Coleman (tp, as, vln); David Izenzon (b); Charles Moffett (d).

Fairfield Hall, Croydon, Surrey, England, August 29, 1965

SADNESS/ CLERGYMAN'S DREAM/ FALLING STARS/ SILENCE/ HAPPY FOOL/ BALLAD/ DOUGH
NUTS

Polydor (Eu) 623246/7, Arista Freedom 1900 (The Great London Concert).
Note: the above double LP also contains tracks by a wind quintet playing Ornette
Coleman's compositions.

CHAPPAQUA SUITE
Ornette Coleman (tp, as); Pharoah Sanders (ts); David Izenzon (b); Charles Moffett
(d) plus eleven brass, woodwind and strings directed by Joseph Tekula.

NYC, June 15/16 & 17, 1965

CHAPPAQUA SUITE part 1, 2, 3, 4

CBS 66203, Columbia (J) 13-14

AT THE GOLDEN CIRCLE
Ornette Coleman (tp, as, vln); David Izenzon (b); Charles Moffett (d).

Golden Circle, Stockholm, Sweden, December 3, 1965

DAWN

Golden Circle, Stockholm, Sweden, December 4, 1965

FACES AND PLACES/ EUROPEAN ECHOES/ DEE DEE

Blue Note BST84224

AT THE GOLDEN CIRCLE – Vol 2:
Ornette Coleman (tp, as, vln); David Izenzon (b); Charles Moffett (d).

Golden Circle, Stockholm, Sweden, December 3, 1965

ANTIQUES/ MORNING SONG

Golden Circle, Stockholm, Sweden, December 4, 1965

SNOWFLAKES AND SUNSHINE/ THE RIDDLE

Blue Note BST84225

THE EMPTY FOXHOLE
Ornette Coleman (tp, as, vln); Charlie Haden (b); Ornette Denardo Coleman (d).

NYC, September 9, 1966

GOOD OLD DAYS/ THE EMPTY FOXHOLE/ SOUND GRAVITATION/ FREEWAY EXPRESS/ FAITHFUL/
ZIG ZAG

Blue Note BST84246

WHO'S CRAZY?
Ornette Coleman (tp, as, vln); David Izenzon (b); Charles Moffett (d, per).

Paris, France, 1966

JANUARY/ SORTIE LE COCUARD/ DANS LA NEIGE/ THE CHANGES/ BETTER GET YOURSELF
ANOTHER SELF/ THE DUEL, TWO PSYCHIC LOVERS AND EATING TIME/ THE MIS-USED BLUES
(The lovers and the alchemist)/ THE POET/ THE WEDDING DAY AND FUZZ/ FUZZ, FEAST,
BREAKOUT, EUROPEAN ECHOES, ALONE AND THE ARREST

Affinity (Eu) AFF 102

THE MUSIC OF ORNETTE COLEMAN

Ornette Coleman (tp) with The Philadelphia Woodwind Quintet.

NYC, March 17, 1967

FORM AND SOUNDS

RCA LPM2982

Note: other titles on the above LP include compositions of Ornette Coleman played by a string quartet.

THE UNPRECEDENTED MUSIC OF ORNETTE COLEMAN

Ornette Coleman (tp, as, shenai); David Izenzon (b); Charlie Haden (b); Ed Blackwell (d). *Rome, Italy, late 1967*

LONELY WOMAN/MONSIEUR LE PRINCE/FORGOTTEN CHILDREN/BUDDHA BLUES

Lotus (Eu) LPPS 11 11 6

NEW YORK IS NOW

Ornette Coleman (tp, as, vln); Dewey Redman (ts); Jimmy Garrison (b); Elvin Jones (d); Mel Fuhrman (vocal interjections). *NYC, April/May 1968*

THE GARDEN OF SOULS/ TOY DANCE/ WE NOW INTERRUPT FOR A COMMERCIAL/ BROADWAY BLUES/ ROUND TRIP

Blue Note BST84287

LOVE CALL

Ornette Coleman (tp, as, vln); Dewey Redman (ts); Jimmy Garrison (b); Elvin Jones (d). *NYC, April/May 1968*

AIRBORNE/ LOVE CALL/ OPEN TO THE PUBLIC/ CHECK OUT TIME

Blue Note BST84356

ORNETTE AT 12

Ornette Coleman (tp, as, vln); Dewey Redman (ts); Charlie Haden (b); Ornette Denardo Coleman (d). *NYC, June 16, 1968*

C.O.D./ RAINBOWS/ NEW YORK/ BELLS AND CHIMES

Impulse AS9178

CRISIS

Don Cherry (tp, Indian flu); Ornette Coleman (as, vln); Dewey Redman (ts); Charlie Haden (b); Ornette Denardo Coleman (d). *NYC, March 22, 1969*

BROKEN SHADOWS/ COMME IL FAUT/ SONG FOR CHE/ SPACE JUNGLE

Impulse AS9187

FRIENDS AND NEIGHBOURS

Ornette Coleman (tp, as, vln); Dewey Redman (ts); Charlie Haden (b); Ed Blackwell (d). *NYC, 1970*

FRIENDS AND NEIGHBOURS/ FRIENDS AND NEIGHBOURS (add vocal)/ LONG TIME NO SEE/ TOMORROW/ FORGOTTEN SONGS

Flying Dutchman FDS123

SCIENCE FICTION
Gerard Schwarg, Carmon Fornarotto (tp); Ornette Coleman (as); Dewey Redman (ts); Charlie Haden (b); Ed Blackwell, Billy Higgins (d); Asha Puthli (vcl).

NYC, September 9, 10 & 13, 1971

WHAT REASON COULD I GIVE/ ALL MY LIFE

Don Cherry (pocket tp); Ornette Coleman (as); Charlie Haden (b); Billy Higgins (d)
CIVILIZATION DAY/ STREET WOMAN

Don Cherry (pocket tp); Bobby Bradford (tp); Ornette Coleman (as); Dewey Redman (ts); Charlie Haden (b); Ed Blackwell, Billy Higgins (d); David Henderson (poet).
SCIENCE FICTION

Ornette Coleman (tp, vln); Dewey Redman (ts, musette); Charlie Haden (b); Ed Blackwell (d).
ROCK THE CLOCK

Bobby Bradford (tp); Ornette Coleman (as); Dewey Redman (ts); Charlie Haden (b); Ed Blackwell (d).
LAW YEARS/ THE JUNGLE IS A SKYSCRAPER

Columbia 31061

SKIES OF AMERICA
Ornette Coleman (as); Dewey Redman (ts, oboe); Charlie Haden (b); Ed Blackwell (d) plus The London Symphony Orchestra conducted by David Measham.

London, England, May, 1972

SKIES OF AMERICA, PART 1: Skies of America/ Native Americans/ The good life/ Birthdays and funerals/ Dreams/ Sounds of sculpture/ Holiday for heroes/ All of my life/ Dancers/ The soul within woman/ The artist in America. SKIES OF AMERICA, PART 2: The new anthem/ Place in space/ Foreigner in a free land/ Silver screen/ Poetry/ The men who live in the White House/ Love life/ The military/ Jam session/ Sunday in America

Columbia KC31562, CBS(Eu)65147

DANCING IN YOUR HEAD
Ornette Coleman (as); Charles Ellerbee, Bern Nix (g); Rudy MacDaniel (b); Ronald Shannon Jackson (d); The Master Musicians of Joujouka; Robert Palmer (cl).

Joujouka, Morocco, January 1973/ Paris, France, December, 1976

THEME FROM A SYMPHONY (Variation 2)/ MIDNIGHT SUNRISE/ THEME FROM A SYMPHONY (Variation 1)

A & M Horizon 722

BODY META
Ornette Coleman (as); Charles Ellerbee, Bern Nix (g); Jamaaladeen Tacuma (elb); Ronald Shannon Jackson (d). *Paris, France, December, 1976*
VOICE POETRY/ HOME GROWN/ MACHO WOMAN/ FOU AMOUR/ EUROPEAN ECHOES
Artists House AH1

SOAPSUDS-SOAPSUDS
Ornette Coleman (tp, ts); Charlie Haden (b). *NYC, January 30, 1977*
MARY HARTMAN MARY HARTMAN/ HUMAN BEING/SOAPSUDS/ SEX SPY/ SOMEDAY
Artists House AH6

OF HUMAN FEELINGS
Ornette Coleman (as); Charles Ellerbee, Bern Nix (g); Jamaaladeen Tacuma (elb); Calvin Weston, Ornette Denardo Coleman (d). *NYC. April 25, 1979*
SLEEP WALK/ JUMP STREET/ HIM AND HER/ AIR SHIP/ WHAT IS THE NAME OF THAT SONG?/ JOB MOB/ LOVE WORDS/ TIMES SQUARE
Antilles ANLP2001

OPENING THE CARAVAN OF DREAMS
Ornette Coleman (as, tp, vln); Bern Nix, Charles Ellerbee (elg); Jamaaladeen Tacuma, Albert McDowell (elb); Ornette Denardo Coleman, Sabir Kamal (d, per).
Fort Worth, Texas, 1985
TO KNOW WHAT TO KNOW/ HARMOLODIC BEBOP/ SEX SPY/ CITY LIVING/ SEE-THRU/ COMPUTE
Caravan of Dreams CD85001

SONG X
Ornette Coleman (as, vln); Pat Metheny (g, g-synth); Charlie Haden (b); Jack DeJohnette (d); Ornette Denardo Coleman (per). *NYC, December 12-14, 1985*
SONG X/MOB JOB/ENDANGERED SPECIES/ VIDEO GAMES/ KATHELIN.GRAY/ TRIGONOMETRY/ SONG X DUO/ LONG TIME NO SEE
Geffen(Eu)924.096-1

IN ALL LANGUAGES
Don Cherry (tp); Ornette Coleman (as, ts); Charlie Haden (b); Billy Higgins (d).
NYC, 1987
PEACE WARRIORS/ FEET MUSIC/ AFRICA IS THE MIRROR OF ALL COLORS/ WORD FOR BIRD/ SPACE CHURCH (Continuous services)/ LATIN GENETICS/ IN ALL LANGUAGES/ SOUND MANUAL/ MOTHERS OF THE VEIL/ CLONING

Ornette Coleman (tp, as); Bern Nix, Charles Ellerbee (elg); Jamaaladeen Tacuma, Albert McDowell (elb); Ornette Denardo Coleman, Calvin Weston (d). *NYC, 1987*
MUSIC NEWS/ MOTHERS OF THE VEIL/ THE ART OF LOVE IS HAPPINESS/ LATIN GENETICS/ TODAY, YESTERDAY AND TOMORROW/ LISTEN UP/FEET MUSIC/ SPACE CHURCH (Continuous services)/ CLONING/ IN ALL LANGUAGES/ BIOSPHERE/ STORY TELLERS/ PEACE WARRIORS
Caravan of Dreams CDP5008

VIRGIN BEAUTY

Ornette Coleman (as, tp, vln); Bern Nix, Charles Ellerbee, Jerry Garcia (g); Chris Walker, Albert McDowell (elb); Ornette Denardo Coleman (keyboard, d, per); Calvin Weston (d).   *1988*

3 WISHES/ BOURGEOIS BOOGIE/ HAPPY HOUR/ VIRGIN BEAUTY/ HEALING THE FEELING/ SINGING IN THE SHOWER/ DESERT PLAYERS/ HONEYMOONERS/ CHANTING/ SPELLING THE ALPHABET/ UNKNOWN ARTIST

Portrait PRT 461193 1

Ornette Coleman on Compact Disc

THE SHAPE OF JAZZ TO COME	Atlantic 19238-2
FREE JAZZ	Atlantic SD1364-2
AT GOLDEN CIRCLE Vol 1	Blue Note CDP84224
AT GOLDEN CIRCLE Vol 2	Blue Note CDP84225
THE MUSIC OF ORNETTE COLEMAN	Bluebird (Eu) ND86561
OF HUMAN FEELINGS	Polystar (J)J33D 20002
IN ALL LANGUAGES	Caravan of Dreams Dreams 008
THE SHAPE OF JAZZ TO COME	Atlantic Jazz K 781339 2
ORNETTE COLEMAN / PAT METHENY: SONG X	Geffen 9240962
VIRGIN BEAUTY	Portrait (Eu) PRT461193 2

Further recordings mentioned in the text

THE LOUIS ARMSTRONG LEGEND 1926-27   World Records (Eu)EG26 0458 1

THE LOUIS ARMSTRONG LEGEND 1927-28   World Records (Eu)SH406

THE LOUIS ARMSTRONG LEGEND 1928-29   World Records (Eu)SH407

LOVIE AUSTIN'S BLUES SERENADERS 1924-26
Tommy Ladnier (cornet); Unknown (tb); Johnny Dodds (cl); Lovie Austin (p);
Eusten Woodfork (banjo). *Chicago, August, 1926*
IN THE ALLEY BLUES
. Fountain (Eu)FJ105

SOLEMN MEDITATION – PAUL BLEY QUARTET
Dave Pike (vbs); Paul Bley (p); Charlie Haden (b); Lennie McBrowne (d).   *LA, 1957*
I REMEMBER HARLEM/ PORGY/ BIRK'S WORKS/ O PLUS ONE/ SOLEMN MEDITATION/ DRUM TWO/
EVERYWHERE/ BEAU DIDDLEY/ PERSIAN VILLAGE
Gene Norman Presents GNPS31

PEE WEE CRAYTON   Charley (Eu) LP105

WORKIN'/ STEAMIN' – MILES DAVIS QUINTET
Miles Davis (tp); John Coltrane (ts); Red Garland (p); Paul Chambers (b); Philly Joe
Jones (d) *New Jersey, May 11, 1956*
IN YOUR OWN SWEET WAY/ DIANE/ TRANE'S BLUES/ SOMETHING I DREAMED LAST NIGHT/
AHMAD'S BLUES – 1/ THE SURREY WITH THE FRINGE ON TOP/ IT NEVER ENTERED MY MIND/
WHEN I FALL IN LOVE/ SALT PEANUTS/ FOUR/ THE THEME 1/ THE THEME 2/
Prestige (Eu) PR 24034
– 1 features rhythm only. PR24034 = Workin' (PR7166) and Steamin' (PR 7200).

CLOSENESS
Ornette Coleman (as); Charlie Haden (b). *NYC, March 21, 1976*
O.C.

Horizon SP710

THE GOLDEN NUMBER
Ornette Coleman (tp); Charlie Haden (b) *NYC, December 19, 1976*
THE GOLDEN NUMBER

Horizon SP727

NEW AND OLD GOSPEL-JACKIE MCLEAN QUINTET
Ornette Coleman (tp); Jackie McLean (as); Lamont Johnson (p); Scott Holt (b); Billy
Higgins (d). *NYC, March 2, 1967*
LIFELINE/ A. OFFSPRING/ B. MIDWAY/ C. VERNZONE/ D. THE INEVITABLE END/ OLD GOSPEL/
STRANGE AS IT SEEMS

Blue Note BST84262

MODERN JAZZ QUARTET
Milt Jackson (vbs); John Lewis (p); Percy Heath (b); Kenny Clarke (d).
NYC, December, 22, 1952
ALL THE THINGS YOU ARE/ LA RONDE/ VENDOME/ ROSE OF THE RIO GRANDE

Milt Jackson (vbs); John Lewis (p); Percy Heath (b); Kenny Clarke (d).
NYC, June 25, 1953
THE QUEEN'S FANCY/ DELAUNAY'S DILEMMA/ AUTUMN IN NEW YORK/ BUT NOT FOR ME

Milt Jackson (vbs); John Lewis (p); Percy Heath (b); Kenny Clarke (d).
NYC, December, 23, 1954

DJANGO/ ONE BASS HIT/ MILANO

Milt Jackson (vbs); John Lewis (p); Percy Heath (b); Kenny Clarke (d).
NYC, January, 9, 1955

LA RONDE SUITE

Milt Jackson (vbs); John Lewis (p); Percy Heath (b); Connie Kay (d).
NYC, July 2, 1955

RALPH'S NEW BLUES/ ALL OF YOU/ GERSHWIN BALLAD MEDLEY/ CONCORDE/ SOFTLY AS IN A
MORNING SUNRISE

Prestige (Eu) PR24005

THELONIOUS MONK TRIO
Thelonious Monk (p); Gary Mapp (b); Art Blakey (d).

NYC, October 15, 1952

LITTLE ROOTIE TOOTIE/ SWEET AND LOVELY/ BYE-YA/ MONKS DREAM

Thelonious Monk (p); Gary Mapp (b); Max Roach (d).

NYC, October 18, 1952

TRINKLE TINKLE/ THESE FOOLISH THINGS/ BEMSHA SWING/ REFLECTIONS

Thelonious Monk (p). *NYC, September 22, 1954*
JUST A GIGOLO

Thelonious Monk (p); Percy Heath (b); Art Blakey (d).
WORK/ NUTTY/ BLUE MONK

Prestige PR7027

CHARLIE PARKER ON DIAL VOL 3-CHARLIE PARKER QUARTET
Charlie Parker (as); Russ Freeman (p); Arnold Fishkin (b); Jimmy Pratt (d).

LA, February 1, 1947

HOME COOKIN' (three takes).

CHARLIE PARKER'S NEW STARS:
Howard McGee (tp); Charlie Parker (as); Wardell Gray (ts); Dodo Marmarosa (p); Barney Kessel (g); Red Callender (b); Don Lamond (d).

LA, February 26, 1947

RELAXIN' AT CAMARILLO (four takes); CHEERS (four takes); CARVIN' THE BIRD (two takes); STUPENDOUS (two takes).

Spotlite (Eu)103

GUNTHER SCHULLER—JAZZ ABSTRACTIONS
NYC, December 20, 1960
. Atlantic LP1365

OUR MAN IN JAZZ – SONNY ROLLINS QUARTET
Don Cherry (cornet); Sonny Rollins (ts); Bob Cranshaw (b); Billy Higgins (d)
NYC, July 29 and 30, 1962

OLEO/ DEARLY BELOVED/ DOXY

RCA (F) 741 091/2

BYRON ALLEN TRIO
Byron Allen (as); Maceo Gilchrist (b); Theodore Robinson (per)

NYC, September 25, 1964

TIME IS PAST/ THREE STEPS IN THE RIGHT DIRECTION/ DECISION FOR THE COLE-MAN/ TODAY'S BLUES TOMORROW

ESP (Disk) 1005

SOUND – ROSCOE MITCHELL SEXTET
Lester Bowie (tp, flugel horn, harmonica); Lester Lashley (tb, cello); Roscoe Mitchell (as, cl, recorder); Maurice McIntyre (ts); Malachi Favors (b); Alvin Fielder (per)

Chicago, August 11 and September 18, 1966

ORNETTE/ THE LITTLE SUITE/ SOUND

Delmark DL 408

OLD AND NEW DREAMS – OLD AND NEW DREAMS
Don Cherry (pocket tp); Dewey Redman (ts); Charlie Haden (b); Ed Blackwell (d)

NYC, October, 1976

HANDWOVEN/ DEWEY'S TUNE/ CHAIRMAN MAO/ NEXT TO THE QUIET STREAM/ AUGMENTED/ OLD AND NEW DREAMS

Black Saint BSR 0013

OLD AND NEW DREAMS – OLD AND NEW DREAMS
Don Cherry (pocket tp/p); Dewey Redman (ts, musette); Charlie Haden (b); Ed Blackwell (d)   *Oslo, Norway, August, 1979*

LONELY WOMAN/ TOGO/ GUINEA/ OPEN OR CLOSE/ ORBIT OF LA-BA/ SONG OF THE WHALES

ECM 1154

OLD AND NEW DREAMS – PLAYING
Don Cherry (pocket tp); Dewey Redman (ts, musette); Charlie Haden (b); Ed Blackwell (d)

Bregenz, Austria, June, 1980

HAPPY HOUSE/ MOPTI/ NEW DREAM/ RUSHOUR/ BROKEN SHADOWS/ PLAYING

ECM 1205